SARAH WILLES

HATTIE DEARDS

RACHEL MARTINO

ANNABEL GRAHAM WOOD

Raw Beet

AGENCY LIMITED

Editor: Hattie Deards
Index compilation: Hattie Deards
Photography: Michelle Moradi www.michellemoradi.com
Food styling: Hattie Deards and Kali Hamm

First Published in the United Kingdom in 2015 by Blues Books www.bluesagency.co.uk

ISBN 978-0-9573955-1-0

Contents

The REAL FOOD SHOP
www.PEPCrealfood.co.uk

Introduction

Diet, knowledge and understanding about food and nutrition couldn't be more polarised than it is at the moment. On the one hand the obesity epidemic is growing worldwide, and we have generations of people who have not been taught the survival skill of simple cooking and food preparation. Yet on the other hand we have access to a more diverse range of foods and ingredients than ever before. Knowledge of food and nutrition has never been better documented and researched, and many people are using innovative methods and technologies to cater for different diets.

Particular diets are in abundance, some for medical reasons, others for nutritional and health reasons, and some out of curiosity. At Blues we're in the privileged position of seeing the changing landscape of food and eating habits. There is a place for every style of diet in our continually changing world, but we have refined things and chosen to focus on four particular groups of recipes:- Gluten free, Raw, Vegan and Low GI.

With the help of our cooks and other contributors, we have tried to put together a collection of fairly simple recipes that can be served formally or informally, using ingredients that can be bought easily. Often 'health' foods can appear unappealing as well as difficult to find, but with the surge of high street health food shops and on-line 'shops' we hope that you will not have any difficulties buying the more specific ingredients.

We have been particularly lucky to work closely with Rachel Martino, a registered nutritional therapist and raw food chef. She inspired us to write this book, and she represents a prominent food movement that is transforming our approach to cookery and eating. Rachel has contributed an abundance of recipes to the book, collaborating with and advising us closely throughout the writing process.

We continue our important work with Blues In Schools, teaching children and adolescents with emotional, behavioural and learning difficulties to cook and have taken immense pride in seeing a number of our students proceed to catering college. We will be contributing a percentage of the proceeds of this book to ensuring that our project continues, and hopefully we will continue to see the pleasure, purpose and pride that cooking can bring about in many of our young people.

Over and above everything we hope that you enjoy the thrill of trying these recipes, and that this book helps you explore some of the different 'diets' that there are out there. While there are many people who need to follow a particular diet for medical reasons, and some who choose to for their own personal reasons, we at Blues have enjoyed gently incorporating the recipes into our daily lives and have found that inadvertently we have altered our attitudes towards ingredients and food, and so the cycle of changing food habits continues. We have all benefitted from expanding our culinary knowledge, and have truly enjoyed moving away from well known, and well loved, recipes.

We'd like to thank all of our cooks and contributors – without your recipes and knowledge we would not have this book. We would also like to thank everyone in the Blues office. We have been testing recipes endlessly and for months we have been relying on the tastebuds and constructive criticism of everyone in the office to guide us in the right direction – thank you Cathy, Katie, Jemma and Ellie.

Foreword

By Prue Leith, CBE, DL

Sarah Willes, who founded Blues nearly forty years ago, is a remarkable woman. Not content with finding jobs for cooks and cooks for jobs, and building up a rightly trusted business, she personally has taught hundreds of children with emotional, learning and behaviour problems to cook, she has written four cookbooks and she has mentored countless young people.

She has also inspired her company with her zeal for Blues in Schools, the charity that came out of her association with Gibbs Green, a special school for troubled children. Many of her staff, and the cooks on her books, give their time to cook with difficult children in school. To the astonishment of their teachers, children unable to concentrate and aggressive in other lessons, nearly always become engaged and happy in the kitchen, – getting on with the job in hand, doing what they are told and ending up having created something that they are justly proud of. Some of them go on to join the catering industry.

Now Blues are doing their bit to tackle another worrying trend: the increase in allergies in children. They have pooled their collective knowledge to come up with exciting, vibrant, imaginative and straightforward recipes for parents, professional cooks and children who need to cook for a raw, vegan, gluten-free or Low GI diet.

Even without the need for "special dietary requirements", I think the recipes in this book will quickly become an inspiration and resource for cooks interested in keeping their repertoire fresh, healthy, up to date and interesting.

I certainly recommend it. Especially as the proceeds will continue to support the admirable Blues In Schools.

Prue Leith

Suppliers

POPS – premium ice popsicles for any special event, made using the finest ingredients, including the champagne ice popsicle and the Bellini popsicle – www.wearepops.com

Vegetarian seaweed caviar – www.vegcaviar.com

Oppo ice cream – healthy indulgent ice cream – www.oppoicecream.co.uk

Tree Harvest – non timber forest products and health foods – www.tree-harvest.com

Goodness Direct – health food supplies – www.goodnessdirect.co.uk

Whole Foods – wide range of quality products from different suppliers – www.wholefoodsmarket.com

As Nature Intended – high street retailer of organic foods and products – www.asnatureintended.uk.com

Planet Organic – wide range of organic food and products – www.planetorganic.com

Field and Flower- Grass fed and free range meat from the Gordano Valley in Somerset delivered to your door – www.fieldandflower.co.uk

The Well Hung Meat Company – grass fed, high welfare meat from local farmers in south Devon delivered to your door – www.wellhungmeat.com

Fish For Thought – Cornish family business delivering fresh fish and seafood straight to your door – www.martins-seafresh.co.uk

Blended Health – individually made juices for your specific health needs, the first targeted juice company on the market – www.blendedhealth.co.uk

Real Food Shop – a mobile village shop selling locally produced foods in the Bridport area of Dorset. www.PEPCrealfood.co.uk

Riverford Organic Farms – organic fruit, vegetables and supplies delivered to your door – www.riverford.co.uk

The Organic Delivery Company – organic fruit, vegetables and groceries from suppliers across the UK delivered to your door – www.theorganicdeliverycompany.co.uk

Conscious Food – providers of award-winning organic health foods of the highest quality, and suppliers of palymyra jaggery sugar substitute – www.consciousfood.co.uk

Hodmedods – British grown grains and pulses, including white quinoa – www.hodmedods.co.uk

The Coconut Collaborative – delicious vegan yoghurts and ice creams made from coconut milk – www.coconutco.co.uk

Tiana – fairtrade and organic certified coconut products – www.tiana-coconut.com

Ideas for your store cupboard

Basic ingredient	Upgrade to consider
Vegetable oil	Coconut Oil and light olive oil
Table salt	Whole sea salt
Wheat flour (thickening sauces)	Arrowroot (cassava) or rice flour if you are on a GF diet
Wheat tortillas	Corn tortillas or rice paper wrappers if you are on a GF diet
White cane sugar	Various alternatives
Salt	Furikake or Gomasio
Croutons	Seeds such as hemp/pumpkin
Milk	Coconut or almond milk if you are following a vegan or dairy free diet
Couscous	Quinoa
Soy sauce	Tamari if you are on a GF diet
Wheat pasta	Brown rice/maize pasta; rice noodles if you are on a GF diet
White rice	Brown or black rice; millet; toasted buckwheat
Cocoa powder	Raw cacao or carob powder

Notes

Throughout the book we have marked each recipe with abbreviations according to which recipe group they fit into. Some recipes fit into every section, others only one or two. The abbreviations are as follows:-

GF – Gluten Free
R – Raw
Low GI – Low Glycaemic Index
V- Vegan
(o) – this indicates that there is an option to make the recipe fit into one of the other categories

Each recipe has a 'suggestions box' alongside it, where we have given serving suggestions and options on how to use alternative ingredients to make the recipe interchangeable across sections.

Where an oven temperature is given in Celsius, we have based this on the oven being fan assisted.

Sugars and natural sweeteners

In this table below you'll find a selection of all the sugars and natural sweeteners used in the book, along with a few other options. Where we indicate R(o), there is a raw option available but this will depend on the brand purchased. We have used an * to indicate the extremely low impact sweeteners in addition to the LGI label.

It's worth a quick mention that there are various forms of sugars from palm trees of all varieties (Palmyra, date & coconut). We have split these into the most common forms available for purchase in the UK, but specific features and nutritional profile will be process/brand dependant.

We have used cane sugar in a couple of our recipes. However, it is our least preferred option, despite being the most readily available.

Dry

Name	GF	R	V	LGI
Coconut sugar	GF	R(o)	V	
Coconut nectar	GF	R	V	LGI
Palmyra Jaggery	GF		V	LGI*
Stevia powder	GF	R(o)	V	LGI*
Xylitol	GF		V	LGI
Cane sugar (brown, white, caster, muscovado)	GF		V	

Syrups / Liquid Sweeteners

Name	GF	R	V	LGI
Coconut nectar	GF	R(o)	V	LGI if raw
Agave syrup	GF	R(o)	V	
Yacon Syrup	GF	R(o)	V	LGI*
Rice syrup	GF		V	
Stevia extract	GF		V	LGI*
Maple syrup	GF		V	
Honey	GF	R(o)		
Date syrup	GF	R(o)	V	

Gluten free food

Gluten free food

Gluten is present in a few very specific foods such as wheat, rye and barley. Oats do not naturally contain gluten, but they easily cross-pollinate with gluten grains, so must be certified gluten free to be considered safe for this diet. Heirloom forms of these grains, such as forms of wheat like spelt and kamut, also contain gluten. In today's world, with so many packaged foods available, gluten is now plentiful.

So what is gluten? In simple terms, it's a protein found in the grains listed above. It's acknowledged as a common allergen and the key culprit to causing ill health in those diagnosed with coeliac disease. For further information on coeliac disease, please refer to Coeliac UK https://www.coeliac.org.uk. Gluten has been known to cause problems to those intolerant to gluten-containing foods. This may manifest as a specific allergy, coeliac disease or intolerance, and in these cases restriction of gluten in the diet is important.

In this chapter we explore a repertoire of delicious gluten-free recipes that are a good addition to any kitchen, whether you are able to eat gluten or not. Please note that in some cases, specific gluten-free ingredients may be required, but in many cases we have focused on naturally gluten-free foods. If you are preparing any of these recipes for someone with an intolerance, allergy or coeliac disease, please give specific attention to the risk of cross contamination of gluten. In these cases, we recommend referencing the resources made available by Coeliac UK, such as ensuring an allergy free workspace, safe cooking utensils and ensuring all ingredients are certified gluten-free.

Spicy garlicky corn on the cob | GF | V | Low GI |

MAKES 4 COBS

- 4 corn on the cob
- 2 garlic cloves
- Pinch of paprika
- Small handful of parsley
- Small handful of coriander
- 1 lemon, juiced
- 1 red chilli
- 2–3 tbsp olive oil

Preheat the oven to 200°C.

Place all the ingredients, apart from the corn, in to a food processor and blitz until it comes together in a wet mixture.

Prepare four separate sheets of tin foil, and place the corn on to each piece of foil. Rub the spicy mix over each cob of corn, and wrap individually into parcels.

Place the corn in the oven for approximately ten minutes, or cook the corn directly on a hot BBQ if you have the chance.

David Renton

These are great to prepare in advance and perfect for any summer barbecue.

Jane's egg free aioli | GF | Low GI |

MAKES 1 JAR

- 90ml whole milk
- 1 tsp Dijon mustard
- 1 garlic clove
- ½ tsp sea salt
- 1 tsp white wine vinegar
- 100ml olive oil
- 80ml sunflower oil
- Black pepper

Put all the ingredients, apart from the oil, into a small blender and whizz until smooth. Add the oils gradually, blending to incorporate all the oil, and scraping down the sides if you need to.

Taste the aioli and add extra salt and pepper if you need to.

Jane O'Brien

Great served with the spicy corn on page 5, or with grilled fish and meat

Edamame bean salsa | GF | V | Low GI |

MAKES 1 MEDIUM BOWL

- 250g frozen edamame beans
- 1 large spring onion
- Handful of fresh coriander
- Handful of fresh mint
- 1½ lemons, juiced
- 4 tbsp extra virgin olive oil + extra to dribble over the salsa
- Sea salt
- Cayenne pepper

Boil the beans in salted water for 5 minutes, and then drain. Tip the beans into a food processor. Top and tail the spring onion, removing any outer leaves and cutting into three pieces. Add the olive oil, lemon juice, spring onion, mint, coriander, pinch of cayenne pepper and a little sea salt.

Turn on the food processor, and whizz together until the ingredients come together. You do not want to blend this to a smooth pulp, you want to maintain a chunky-ish texture.

Check the seasoning, and decant to a bowl. Pour over some additional olive oil before serving.

Serve with a hearty slice of toasted bread for a protein filled and satisfying lunch.

Blues

Serve with gluten free crackers or gluten free bread.

Carrot humous | GF |

MAKES ONE MEDIUM SIZED BOWL

- 750g carrots, peeled
- 2 tsp coriander seeds
- 1 ½ tsp caraway seeds
- 50ml rapeseed oil
- 4 cloves of garlic
- 2 sprigs of thyme
- 25ml rapeseed oil
- 1–2 tsp honey
- 4 tbsp tahini
- 2 lemons, juiced
- Fresh red chilli
- Fresh coriander

Pre-heat the oven 200°C.

Peel the carrots and slice them into 2cm disks. Put the carrots into a baking tray, sprinkle over the coriander seeds, the caraway seeds and season with salt and pepper. Add the thyme, the peeled garlic cloves and a glass of tap water. Cover the baking tray with tin foil and place in the oven, and cook for 30–40 minutes, or until the carrots are soft. Transfer to a mixing bowl to cool down, covering with cling film to keep in the steam for a few minutes while you prepare the food processor.

Tip the carrots into a food processor. Add the rapeseed oil, honey, tahini and the juice of 2 lemons. Blend all the ingredients together, and taste. Add salt and pepper if you need to. If the humous is too thick, add a little water and blend to the right consistency.

Decant the humous into a serving bowl. Garnish with coriander leaves and some chopped fresh red chilli.

Oliver Gladwin

Low Gl (o) – take out the honey or replace it with maple syrup.
V (o) – take out the honey, or replace it with maple syrup.
Great with gluten free oat cakes, or served with a baked potato and salad.

Grilled red pepper and almond dip | GF |

- 1 large red pepper
- 3 dried figs
- 2 fillets of anchovy in olive oil
- 15 whole blanched almonds
- 1–2tbsp olive oil
- 1 clove of garlic, crushed
- 1 small red chilli
- Juice of ½ a lemon

Grill the red pepper until its skin is blistered, and place it into a plastic bag for a while, until you are able to peel off the skin and remove the seeds.

Soak the figs in some warm water and pinch off the stems.

Put all the ingredients into a food processor and whizz for just a few minutes, so that the texture remains just slightly rough.

Check the seasoning. The flavour should be slightly sweet from the figs, with a twist of bitter from the lemon juice.

This dip is best eaten the next day, to allow the flavours to fully develop.

Pim Phillips

Great with gluten free oatcakes, crudité, chunks of grilled polenta or roasted sweet potatoes.

Pim's pomegranate yoghurt | GF | Low GI |

- 500ml plain yoghurt
- 80–100g Pomegranate seeds
- 30g finely chopped mint
- 1 tsp garam masala
- Pinch of salt, optional

Mix together all the ingredients in a large bowl, keeping aside a few of the pomegranate seeds to scatter over the top just before serving.

V (0) – use plain coconut yoghurt to make this vegan. This refreshing yoghurt can be served as a dip, or as an accompaniment to any curry.

Healthy fiery chicken salad | GF |

SERVES 6

- 200g daikon, peeled and sliced into matchsticks
- 1 carrot, peeled and sliced into thin matchsticks
- ½ red onion, finely sliced
- 500g chicken skinless chicken thighs, poached or steamed, and then shredded
- 2 large handfuls of mint, picked
- 100g bean sprouts
- 1 shallot, finely chopped
- 100g peanuts, roughly broken up
- 1½ tbsp olive oil to fry the shallots and peanuts
- 30ml vegetable oil
- 30ml rice vinegar
- 2 tsp nuom mam (fish sauce)
- Juice of 1 lime
- 1 tbsp palm sugar
- 1 red chilli, finely chopped
- 15g root ginger grated
- 1 garlic clove, diced

Pre-heat the oven to 190°C.

Make a tin foil parcel around the chicken thighs with enough room to allow the steam to gather around the chicken. Steam the chicken for 20 minutes or until just cooked. Alternatively you can poach the thighs in simmering water for 10–15 minutes. Set the chicken aside.

To make the dressing, dissolve the palm sugar in the fish sauce, heating the fish sauce in a small pan if need be. Measure out the vegetable oil and rice vinegar in a measuring jug. Add the fish sauce, palm sugar, lime juice, red chilli, garlic, ginger and diced shallot. Set the dressing aside to develop a good flavour.

Using a very sharp knife cut the carrots and daikon into thin match sticks. Tip them into a large salad bowl. Add the thinly sliced red onion, the bean sprouts, the shredded chicken and tear in plenty of fresh mint.

In a heavy bottomed frying pan, heat the olive oil. Fry the finely chopped shallot until turning golden. Add the broken up peanuts and fry until they are nicely toasted. Tip the shallots and peanuts on to some kitchen paper to cool for a few minutes, and then tip them into the salad bowl.

When you are ready to eat, pour over the dressing. Mix up the salad and dressing with your hands, add any left over mint leaves and serve immediately.

Sam Watherston

Low GI (o) – replace the palm sugar with Palmyra Jaggery nectar.

Red pepper and freekeh pilaf | Low GI |

SERVES 4–6 PEOPLE

- 3 tbsp olive oil
- 4–5 banana shallots
- 4 cloves garlic
- 4 red peppers
- 2 bay leaves
- 250g freekeh, or a mix of 125g freekeh and 125g quinoa for a lighter pilaf
- 500ml vegetable or chicken stock
- 60g pumpkin seeds, toasted in a dry pan
- Small bunch of flat leaf parsley, roughly chopped
- Sea salt and black pepper

Peel the shallots and slice them thinly into circles. Peel and thinly slice the garlic.

Wash the peppers, remove the seeds and thin into thin strips.

Heat the olive oil in a large thick bottomed saucepan or a saute pan. Add the shallots and cook for 5 minutes on a moderate heat, making sure that they don't catch. Add the peppers and the garlic. Stir well and add a good grind of pepper along with a pinch of salt and the bay leaves. Stir well, and allow to cook for a further 5 minutes.

Add the freekeh to the pan and stir in well. Add the stock, and leave the pilaf to bubble gently for approximately 15 minutes or until the grain is cooked, stirring every now and then to make sure it doesn't stick. The freekeh should absorb the majority of the water, but not be dry in any way. It should have a loose risotto consistency.

Toast the pumpkin seeds in a dry pan until they have just gained some colour. Tip them into the pilaf along with the chopped parsley and stir in with a large serving spoon. Check the seasoning, and adjust if you need to. Serve when warm but not scolding hot.

Delicious served with the Emerald Green Salad on page 39.

Hattie Deards

V (o) – use vegetable instead of chicken stock.

Leek, celery and cannellini bean soup | GF | Low GI |

SERVES 6–8

- 2 × drained tins of cannellini beans
- 3 tbsp olive oil
- 2 leeks, thinly sliced
- 2 celery stalks, thinly sliced
- 2 diced carrots
- 80g Italian risotto rice
- 2 or 3 sprigs of thyme
- 4 heaped tsp tomato puree
- 1 courgette, thinly sliced
- 1 litre of gluten free vegetable or chicken stock
- Small sweetheart or savoy cabbage, very finely shredded
- 250g fresh spinach
- 2 lemons, juiced
- Sea salt and black pepper
- Parmesan or pecorino shavings – optional

Drain and rinse the tinned cannellini beans, and set aside.

Thinly slice the leeks, celery and dice the carrots. Slice the courgette, and set it aside.

Heat the olive oil in a large heavy bottomed pan. Add the leeks, celery and carrot to the pan, and cook over a medium heat for 5 minutes. Add the risotto rice and the thyme, and stir well. Pour 500ml of stock in to the pan and allow to simmer for 10 minutes. Add the tomato puree, the sliced courgette and finely shredded cabbage and simmer for a further 10 minutes, adding more stock in stages.

When the cabbage and courgettes are cooked through, add the spinach and cook for a few minutes, until it is wilted. Add the cannellini beans and the lemon juice, and season with salt and pepper.

When you are about to serve the soup, shave some parmesan over the soup with a vegetable peeler.

Serve with fresh gluten free bread on page 26 or the cornbread on page 32.

Blues

Vegan (o) – use vegetable stock and replace the parmesan cheese with nutritional yeast, or omit it altogether.

Sarah's green vietnamese soup | GF |

SERVES 4–6

- 3 tbsp ground nut oil or vegetable oil
- 4 spring onions, sliced finely
- 1 medium piece of ginger, peeled
- 5 lime leaves, fresh or frozen, and finely sliced
- 2 sticks of lemon grass
- 1 to 2 green chillies
- 1 clove of garlic
- 1 tin coconut milk, using just the coconut water, not the cream
- 2 limes, juice and zest of both
- 2 tbsp of fish sauce
- 1.7 litres of vegetable stock
- 150g french beans, cut into chunks
- 150g edamame beans
- 150g broccoli, cut into small florets
- 150g mange tout
- Half a bunch of fresh coriander
- Pinch of sugar, to taste

Finely slice the spring onions, ginger, lime leaves, lemon grass, chillis and the garlic . Heat the oil in a large saucepan or deep wok, and add the sliced ingredients, gently frying for 4 to 5 minutes.

Strain the coconut water from the coconut milk. Add the water to the pan along with the juice of 2 limes, the fish sauce and the vegetable stock. When the liquid is hot, add the green beans and simmer for 2 minutes. Add the edamame beans and broccoli, and cook for a further 3 minutes. Finally add the mange tout and cook for a further minute.

Check the seasoning and add a pinch of sugar if needed, and serve with chopped fresh coriander. Serve immediately so that the vegetables keep their fresh green colour.

Sarah Willes

Low GI (o) – use a sugar substitute instead of cane sugar.
V (o) – replace the fish sauce with dulse flakes.

Prawns with black rice noodles and miso dressing | GF | Low GI |

SERVES 4

- 3 tbsp brown rice miso
- 1 large clove garlic, crushed
- 2 inches ginger, finely grated
- 3 tbsp mirin
- 3 limes, juiced
- 4 tbsp sesame oil
- 2 tbsp rapeseed oil + 1 tbsp extra
- 200g folded rice noodles, or black rice noodles if you can find them
- 240g raw peeled king prawns
- 125g shitake mushrooms
- 100g babycorn
- 100g mange tout
- Handful mixed dried seaweed salad
- 10 radishes, sliced
- 8 spring onions sliced
- 2 red chillis sliced
- Small bunch Thai basil and coriander
- 1 tbsp gluten free tamari soy sauce
- Dried red chilli flakes, or Ichimi Togarashi
- Sea salt

Make the dressing first. Peel and crush the garlic and add it to a large bowl or jug. Peel the ginger and grate it, and add it to the garlic. Add the miso, mirin, lime juice and stir thoroughly. Slowly add the sesame oil and rapeseed oil while continually mixing to emulsify the dressing, and set aside.

Bring a large pan of water to the boil and add the noodles. Turn the heat off, stir the noodles every now and then so that they don't stick, and let the hot water soften the noodles to the right consistency, which should take around 5 minutes. They can very easily over cook, so drain them the minute they feel soft. Run them under cold water, shake and tip into a large mixing bowl with a little sesame oil so that they don't stick together.

Rehydrate your seaweed by covering it with water and leaving it to sit for ten minutes. Poach your prawns by bringing a small saucepan of water to a gentle simmer. Add the prawns and cook gently for about 3–4 minutes, until the prawns turn pink and are just cooked. Drain and set aside.

Heat one tablespoon of rapeseed oil in a frying pan. When the oil is hot add the shitake mushrooms and pan fry them on a medium to high heat. Sprinkle over a little sea salt and stir regularly. When they are cooked and a little browned in areas, tip them onto a plate and set aside. Add a little water to the same pan. Cut the baby corn into chunks on the diagonal, along with the mange touts and add them into the pan to steam/pan fry for no more than 2 minutes. Ensuring that your vegetables are still crunchy tip them on to the plate with the mushrooms and set aside.

Add the vegetables to the mixing bowl with the noodles. Add the sliced radishes, sliced spring onions (reserving a few for garnish), the sliced red chilli, half the prawns and the seaweed. Tip in the dressing and using your hands mix together all the ingredients. Roughly chop the coriander and basil, add the herbs to the bowl and mix through with a splash of tamari soy sauce (adding , adding more lime if you like. Garnish with remaining prawns, spring onion, a drizzle of sesame oil, and a sprinkle of Ichimi Togarashi or dried chilli flakes.

*Black Rice noodles are available from some Asian grocery stores and Wholefoods. All other Asian ingredients available at Asian grocery stores.

Kali Hamm

Black rice noodles are available from some Asian stores and Wholefoods.

Kedgeree | GF | Low GI |

SERVES 4

- 500g smoked haddock, salmon, kippers or a mixture of whatever fish you like
- 2 bay leaves
- 2 tbsp olive oil
- 1 large onion
- 175g long grain rice or brown rice
- 2 tsp curry powder (ensure that it is gluten free)
- 3 hard boiled eggs, chopped
- 12 or more fresh prawns, optional
- 50g butter
- 1 bunch of parsley, chopped
- Juice of 1 lemon

Add approximately 1 litre of water to a shallow pan. Add the bay leaf and the parsley stalks, and bring the water to a gentle boil. Turn it down to a very slight simmer, and add the fish, cut into 4 pieces if necessary. Gently poach the fish for 6 to 7 minutes, until the flesh is just cooked. Using a slotted spoon, remove the fish from the water and set it aside on a plate, covering it with foil, and keep the poaching water to use later.

Chop the onion finely. Heat the olive oil in a thick bottomed pan, add the onion and allow it to cook until transparent. Add the curry powder, stir well and add the rice. Pour over roughly 600ml of the poached fish water, stir well and cook the rice steadily, adding more fish water if you need to, until the rice is just cooked and has absorbed the water.

Carefully remove any skin from the poached fish, remove any bones and flake the fish. If you are using prawns, make sure that they are already cooked, and add the fish and prawns to the rice. Add chopped parsley, the butter and the juice of one lemon.

Using a large metal spoon, mix together all the ingredients. Season with salt and pepper. The kedgeree should have a buttery lemony taste, so add more lemon juice if need be.

Finally add the chopped egg, and serve with a large bowl of steaming peas.

Hattie Deards

Slow roasted shoulder of lamb with sprout tops, finely sliced cabbage and butternut squash puree | GF | Low GI |

SERVES 6

- 1 whole shoulder of lamb
- 4 tbsp olive oil
- 2 onions, roughly chopped
- 2 sticks of celery, chopped into slices
- 4 cloves of garlic
- 1 bunch of fresh thyme
- 500ml lamb stock
- 2 butternut squash
- 1 orange
- 2 tbsp crème fraiche
- 1 small savoy cabbage
- 4 sprout tops or 400g sprouts
- Sea salt and black pepper

Preheat the oven to 160°C.

Remove your shoulder of lamb from the fridge well in advance, allowing for it to come up to room temperature.

Heat two tablespoons of olive oil in a frying pan, add the onions and celery and gently fry them for 5 minutes, then transfer them into a casserole or roasting tray large enough to fit the lamb. Peel the cloves of garlic and add them to the onions, and add the stalks of thyme, keeping aside 4 sprigs to use for the squash.

Rub 1 tablespoon of olive oil over the lamb. Heat a large frying pan and quickly seal the shoulder of lamb, skin side down. Transfer the lamb to the casserole or roasting tray, placing it skin side up on top of the onions, celery, garlic and thyme. Season the lamb with salt and pepper.

Pour the meat stock around the meat and seal it firmly with a lid or thick tin foil. Place the dish in the oven and leave it to cook slowly for approximately 4 hours. By this time the meat should be falling away from the bones and be very soft. Tip the juices into a jug, and leave them to separate so that you can spoon off the fat. Once the juices are free of the fat, season the juice if it needs it.

While the lamb is cooking cut the squash in half, remove the seeds, rub well with olive oil and season with salt and pepper. Wrap the squash halves up in tin foil, and place in the oven to cook for 2 hours, until they are soft. Scoop out the flesh of the squash and put it into a food processor, along with the zest and juice of one orange and the crème fraiche. Blitz together to make a puree.

When you are ready to eat, finely slice the savoy cabbage and sprout tops / sprouts. Steam the vegetables until just done, and still a vibrant green. Drain, add salt and pepper, and serve immediately with the lamb.

Sarah Willes

Pho Bo – Vietnamese beef and noodle soup | GF |

SERVES 4

- 1 large piece of ginger
- 1 large bulb of garlic
- 3 roasted shallots, halved
- 1 large onion
- 2k or more of beef bones
- 5 star anise
- 1 small cinnamon stick
- Sea salt and black pepper
- 3 tbsp gluten free fish sauce
- 1 tbsp coconut sugar or palm sugar
- 200g rice noodles
- 300g beef fillet
- 50g bean sprouts
- 50g Thai basil or normal basil, chopped
- 50g fresh coriander, chopped
- 50g spring onions
- 2 limes cut into wedges
- Chilli paste to taste
- 2 fresh hot red chillis – optional
- Soy sauce to taste

Preheat the oven to 190°C.

Roast the ginger, garlic, onion and shallots until quite dark.

Bring two large pans of water to the boil. Add the beef bones to one pan and cook for 5 minutes, then remove the bones and discard the water. Place the bones into the second pan of boiling water, add the roasted vegetables plus the star anise, cinnamon, salt, pepper, fish sauce and sugar.

Cook gently over a low heat for approximately 3 to 5 hours. Sieve the stock into a large bowl, discard the bones and roasted vegetables. Allow the stock to cool completely before skimming off the fat. It can be reduced further, and seasoned with more fish sauce, and salt & pepper, if need be.

When you are ready to eat gently heat the stock and check the seasoning. Cook the noodles in a pan of boiling water, according to manufacturers instructions, drain and set aside.

Slice the beef fillet into thin strips, and slide it into the pan of hot stock. Allow it to simmer for a minute before adding the noodles, along with the spring onions. Scatter over the chopped herbs and bean sprouts, serve with a wedge of lime and some chilli paste and fresh chillis, if you wish to use them, and add soy sauce to taste.

This soup is so versatile that you can add tofu, chicken and whatever vegetables you may have to hand, and obviously can be made well in advance which makes it a good soup when you are cooking for friends.

Pip McKellar

Southeast asian style roasted salmon | GF |

SERVES 6

- 800g salmon fillet
- 60ml (gluten free) fish sauce
- 75ml mirin rice wine or white wine
- 2 cloves of garlic, peeled and crushed
- 2 tsp finely grated fresh ginger
- 1 tbsp brown sugar or coconut sugar
- Juice of 2 large limes
- Large bunch of fresh coriander

Pre-heat the oven to 200°C.

Line a large baking tray with oiled tin foil. Place the salmon, skin side down, on to the foil and fold up the edges slightly. Season the fish with salt and pepper.

In a small pan mix together the fish sauce, mirin, garlic, ginger and brown sugar. Heat the sauce until it is boiling, and leave it to simmer and thicken for a few minutes.

Pour the sauce over the salmon and place it in the oven to cook for 20 to 25 minutes, until the fillet is just cooked. The sauce may taste very strong at this point, but it mellows with the lime juice that is added at the end.

When cooked, place the salmon on to a large serving plate and spoon over the sauce. Squeeze over the juice of the limes and scatter over plenty of chopped coriander.

This salmon can be eaten hot with rice or noodles, or is excellent eaten cold with salads.

Annabel Graham-Wood

Pan fried seabass with chorizo and clams | GF | Low GI |

SERVES 4

- 4 bass fillets
- 2 fennel bulbs
- 100ml of white wine
- 130g diced raw chorizo (ensure that it is gluten free)
- Large handful of clams, optional
- 150ml cream
- Handful of chopped parsley
- 4 tbsp olive oil
- Sea salt and black pepper

Pre-heat the oven to 170°C.

Wash and clean the clams if you are using them, and set aside.

Slice the fennel bulbs into thick strips lengthways. Heat a griddle pan or frying pan to a high heat on the hob, and chargrill the sliced fennel for a few minutes on each side in the dry pan. Remove the fennel from the pan, drizzle over 2 tablespoons of olive oil, season with salt and pepper, and roast in the oven for 10 to 15 minutes or until soft, and then set aside.

Cook the diced chorizo in a pan on a low heat for 5 to 10 minutes, allowing the delicious paprika oils to be released and the sausage to be cooked through.

In the meantime rub the skin of the sea bass with the remaining 2 tablespoons of olive oil, and season with salt and pepper. In a separate pan, fry the fish skin side down for 4 minutes, turn over a cook for a further few minutes.

While the fish is cooking, add the wine to the chorizo, and reduce for a few minutes. Add the cleaned clams – if you are using them – and allow the clams to cook and open. Reduce the heat, pour over the cream, cover and cook for a further 3 minutes or until the clams fully open.

Plate up the fennel, add the sea bass to each plate and spoon over the clams, cream and chorizo. Scatter over the chopped parsley, and season with salt and pepper.

Serve with fresh green beans, shredded spring greens or sliced sprout tops.

Carina Sage

Asparagus, butterbean and mozzarella salad | GF | Low GI |

SERVES 4

- 400g tin of butter beans or borlotti beans, drained
- 350g raw green asparagus
- 1 lemon, juiced and zest of ½ the lemon
- Small handful of fresh thyme or oregano
- 4 tbsp extra virgin olive oil
- 1 large red bell pepper, sliced into thin match sticks
- 300g buffalo mozzarella, torn roughly
- Sea salt and black pepper

Drain the tin of beans and tip them into a large salad bowl.

Break any woody stalks off the end of the asparagus, and rinse them under the tap. Thinly slice the raw asparagus on the diagonal, trying to keep them as delicate as possible. Add the asparagus to the beans, and add the thinly sliced red pepper.

Add the lemon zest, lemon juice and olive oil, and stir the salad well. Scatter over the thyme leaves, and season with sea salt and black pepper, before stirring again to make sure everything is well dressed.

When you are ready to serve your salad, scatter over the mozzarella.

Hattie Deards

Veggie burgers with a lime leaf yogurt sauce | GF | Low GI |

MAKES 6 BURGERS

- 350g sweet potatoes, peeled and grated
- 300g courgettes, grated
- 225g ground almonds
- 2 eggs
- 2 tbsp smoked paprika
- 1 tbsp oregano or thyme (fresh or dried) finely chopped.
- 1.5 tbsp light olive oil for frying
- 250g pot of low fat Greek yoghurt
- 2 kaffir lime leaves
- zest and juice of 1 lemon
- ½ tbsp extra virgin olive oil
- Sea salt and black pepper

Peel the sweet potatoes and grate manually, or with a food processor, and then tip into a large mixing bowl. Cut the ends off the courgettes, grate them and add to the bowl. Add all the ingredients into a bowl and mix together. Add the almonds, eggs, paprika, oregano and salt and pepper. Stir the mixture up really thoroughly, and using your hands make sure that all the ingredients are well blended. Still using your hands mould the mixture into 12 balls and press into flat patty shapes. Lay these on to some greaseproof paper on a baking tray and place in the fridge to firm up for as long as you can.

For the sauce, tip the yoghurt into a mixing bowl. Using a pestle and mortar (or the end of a rolling pin) bash the kaffir lime leaves until completely broken up into tiny pieces, and add it to the yoghurt along with the lemon juice, zest and olive oil. Mix well.

Add the light olive oil to a large non-stick frying pan and heat. Gently fry the burgers (in batches if necessary) until they are golden and crispy on each side.

Serve the burgers hot or cold with the yoghurt sauce, and a green salad.

Alice Dewey

Serve with toasted gluten free white bread, recipe on page 26.

Gluten free white yeast bread | GF |

MAKES 1 LOAF

- 250g rice flour
- 110g fine cornmeal
- 2 ½ tsp xantham gum
- 1 ½ tsp salt
- 50g dried milk powder
- 85g caster sugar
- 5 tsp dried yeast powder
- 3 free-range eggs, medium-sized
- 300ml warm water
- 1 tsp white wine vinegar
- 2lb / 1 kilo loaf tin

Preheat the oven to 190°C.

In a large mixing bowl combine all the dry ingredients and mix well together. Gluten-free flours are very fine and need to be very well blended before any liquid is added.

Whisk the eggs, add the water and white wine vinegar, and mix well.

Gradually add the liquid to the dry ingredients and beat well for approximately 10 minutes, preferably using an electric mixer, as the consistency of the mixture is too wet to knead by hand.

Spoon the mixture into a well oiled loaf tin and cover with a clean tea towel. Allow the dough to rise to just over the level of the tin. Bake for 45 minutes, remove from the tin and bake for a further 5–10 minutes until the bread sounds hollow when tapped.

Tim Allen
The Ballymaloe Bread Book
Gill & Macmillan Ltd 2001

Forager's wild blackberry muffins | GF |

- 1 tsp flax seed or chia seeds, hydrated in 45g of warm water
- 200g rice flour
- 30g buckwheat flour
- 30g arrowroot or tapioca flour
- 25g ground almonds
- 15g gluten free baking powder
- ½ tsp cinnamon
- Pinch of sea salt
- 125ml of maple syrup or coconut nectar
- 250g almond milk or normal milk
- 2 tsp cider vinegar
- 375g wild blackberries
- Flaked almonds

Pre-heat the oven to 160°C.

If you want to use paper muffin cases lay them out on a muffin tray, or you can simply pour the batter straight into a non-stick muffin tin.

Put the flax or chia seeds into a small cup or bowl, cover with the water and set aside to hydrate.

Tip the rice flour, buckwheat flour, arrowroot, ground almonds, baking powder, cinnamon and sea salt into a large mixing bowl, and mix together the ingredients with a whisk.

In a separate bowl whisk together the flaxseeds/chia seeds, maple syrup, the milk and the vinegar. Mix well to make sure that everything is incorporated, then slowly add this mixture to the dry ingredients, stirring thoroughly to ensure that there are no lumps.

Gently fold the blackberries into the batter, and spoon the mixture into the muffin tin or cases. Sprinkle over some flaked almonds, and put them straight into the oven.

Bake for approximately 20 minutes, until golden brown. Allow the muffins to cool in the tin for 10 minutes before removing them and putting them on a rack.

Herve Leber

Vegan (o) – use almond milk instead of normal milk.

Vanilla tapioca with mangoes in passion fruit syrup | GF | Low GI |

SERVES 4–6

- 60g xylitol
- 4 ripe passion fruit
- 2 ripe mangoes
- 130g tapioca
- 1 litre whole milk or coconut milk
- 1 vanilla pod

Peel the mangoes and cut the flesh into fine slices and place them in a mixing bowl. Cut the ripe passion fruits in half and scoop the seeds and flesh over the mango. Sprinkle over a teaspoon of xylitol and set aside.

Place the tapioca, milk and xylitol into a large saucepan. Split the vanilla pod lengthways, scrape out the seeds and add them to the pan along with the pod. Stir the pan over a low heat for 30–35 minutes, making sure that it does not catch on the bottom. It will seem very milky, but the tapioca will expand, and can easily stick to the bottom of the pan. When cooked the tapioca should be thick-ish and creamy, with a slight bite to the pearls.

Remove the vanilla pod and pour the tapioca equally between individual bowls, or into one large serving bowl. Cover with cling film and leave to cool completely. Before you are ready to serve the tapioca arrange the mango slices over, and pour over the passion fruit seeds and juice.

If you like a particularly creamy pudding, substitute 300ml of whole milk for cream.

Sarah Willes

Vegan (o) – use coconut milk instead of whole milk.

Rose geranium and raspberry jelly | GF |

MAKES 6 INDIVIDUAL DARIOLE MOULDS OR ONE MEDIUM SIZED BOWL

- 200ml water
- 180g agave syrup
- 1 lemon, juiced
- 10 rose geranium leaves/ pelargonium leaves, thinly sliced
- 160g blueberries
- 5 leaves of gelatine, softened in water
- 540g fresh raspberries
- 1 lemon, juiced
- 3 tbsp agave syrup
- 2 leaves of gelatine

Mix together the water, agave syrup and juice of one lemon in a mixing bowl. Thinly slice the geranium leaves, add them to the mix and set aside.

Soften the gelatine leaves in a small bowl with a little water. This should take a couple of minutes. When the gelatine is soft and wobbly, pick it out of the water and put it straight into a small sauce pan. Melt it over a very low heat, which should take a matter of seconds. When it is melted, pour the water mix into the pan and stir well. Set the pan aside for 10 minutes to cool a little.

Scatter the blueberries into the bowl that you wish to use, or if you are using dariole moulds divide the blueberries equally between each mould. Carefully pour the rose geranium jelly mix into the bowl or the dariole moulds, dividing the mixture as equally as possible.

Place the jellies into the fridge to cool straight away.

While the first layer of the jelly is setting make the raspberry puree. Tip the raspberries into a medium sized pan. Add the lemon juice and agave syrup, and heat over a medium heat, stirring occasionally. Allow the raspberries to bubble gently for approximately 15 minutes, until they are completely broken down and start to thicken slightly.

Hold a sieve over a clean bowl, and strain through the raspberries, removing all pips and fibres. Taste the puree, and add more agave syrup if too sharp. Allow the puree to cool.

Again, soak the gelatine in water, then add to a small pan and melt completely. Add the raspberry mixture, stir well, and set aside to cool.

When you are sure that the geranium layer has set in the bowl or moulds, carefully pour over the raspberry jelly mix, dividing it equally between the moulds. Place the jellies in to the fridge and allow to set firmly before serving.

When you are ready to serve, dip the base of the moulds in to hot water and turn them out, so that the clear geranium jelly is at the top, with the raspberry jelly as the underneath layer.

Oliver Gladwin

This archetypal English pudding perfectly reflects Olly's core belief that what grows together goes together.

Sunshine seville orange cup cakes | GF |

- 2 eggs
- 150g coconut sugar
- 200g finely grated peeled sweet potato
- 100g white rice flour
- 100g ground almonds
- 2 tsp baking powder
- 4 tsp marmalade
- 250g mascarpone
- 3 tbsp agave syrup

Pre heat the oven to 175°C.

Crack the eggs into a large mixing bowl. Whisk the eggs with an electric whisk for a few minutes, add the sugar and continue to whisk for a further minute until light and frothy.

Fold in the sweet potato, rice flour, almonds, baking powder and 2 tsp marmalade, and mix well.

Spoon the mixture into cake cases or a non-stick muffin tray, and cook for 15 minutes or until just firm. If you are using metal tin tray moulds, be aware that the cup cakes will cook more quickly.

Spoon the mascarpone into a clean mixing bowl. Add the agave syrup and the marmalade, and gently mix it all together. Be careful to mix the mascarpone gently, otherwise it can split and go gritty. Check the taste and add more agave syrup if it is too sharp.

If you are making chocolate or raspberry, omit the marmalade and add 2 to 3 teaspoons of raw cacao powder or dehydrated raspberry powder.

Once the cakes have cooled, pipe the icing on to the top of the cakes.

Sarah Willes

These cakes keep well for up to 4 days in an airtight container.

Cornbread | GF |

SERVES 6

- A little butter for greasing
- 250g fine cornmeal or maize meal
- 2 tsp (gluten free) baking powder
- ½ tsp (gluten free) bicarbonate of soda
- 1 tsp fine salt
- 100ml plain whole-milk yoghurt
- 200ml whole milk
- 75g grated parmesan – optional

Heat the oven to 200°C.

Butter a loaf tin.

In a large bowl, mix together the cornmeal, baking powder, bicarbonate of soda and salt. Whisk together the milk and yoghurt, and stir into the mix along with the parmesan, and mix thoroughly.

Pour into the tin and bake for 25 minutes, until firm and golden on top. Leave to cool a little, and serve while still warm.

Hattie Deards

Red zest | GF |

SERVES 4

- 6 blood oranges
- 1 pomegranate
- 1 bunch of basil
- 250g tub of mascarpone
- 1 tbsp crème fraiche
- 2 tsp agave syrup
- 1 lemon, grated zest

Using a sharp knife, remove the peel of the orange, ensuring all the white pith is removed. Cut the oranges into thin slices, and arrange them on a plate.

Cut open the pomegranate, and using your hands to remove the seeds, ensuring that none of the white pith stays on the seeds. Scatter the seeds over the sliced oranges.

Combine the crème fraiche, mascarpone, lemon zest and the agave syrup.

When you are ready to serve, tear the basil over the oranges, and serve with a spoonful of the lemon cream on the side.

Blues

Raw food

Raw food

Have you ever had an apple straight from the tree? Crisp, just like a beautiful autumn morning, sweet and crunchy.

When we say *raw food* we are referring to vegan food which has not been treated with heat over 42°C or 105°F. This is a general threshold, past which certain nutrients begin to significantly diminish or disappear, so is used as a general benchmark.

In this chapter we explore a variety of specific culinary techniques which enhance food in its most natural, raw form. We found techniques such as marinating, spiralizing and blending to be particularly effective. These techniques are not limited to raw food preparation of course.

Some individuals choose to eat a 100% raw food diet, and many others choose to simply add a selection to an otherwise standard diet. You may notice as well, that in this chapter many dishes also naturally embody the other principles explored in this book. Feel free to mix and match at your leisure.

Rachel's creamy dressing or dip | R | V | GF | Low GI |

- 60g cashew nuts
- 15g hemp seeds
- 1 lemon, juiced
- 1 piece of dulse
- 1 tbsp olive oil
- 1 tsp nutritional yeast
- Pinch of sea salt
- 1 handful of fresh herbs, optional

Put all the ingredients into a spice grinder or a high speed blender and blitz together until you have a relatively smooth dressing. This is also delicious as a dip.

Rachel Martino

Perfect with seasonal greens and cucumber. If you are not 100% raw, try serving this with roasted sweet potato.

Sumac and avocado dressing | R | V | GF |

- 1 avocado
- 2 satsumas, juiced
- ½ tsp sumac
- ½ tsp turmeric, fresh or ground
- A pinch of sea salt

Put all the ingredients in to a blender and whizz together to make a smooth, creamy dressing.

Rachel Martino

Use as a dressing for salads or as a dip for raw vegetables. Delicious with toasted rye bread, if you are not 100% raw.

Cheesy seedy topping | R | GF | Low GI |

MAKES: 1 SMALL JAR

- 70g cashews
- 2 tbsp flax seeds
- 1 tbsp hemp seeds
- ½ tsp turmeric
- Pinch cayenne pepper
- Pinch of black pepper
- 2 tbsp nutritional yeast
- Pinch sea salt

Put all ingredients in spice grinder or high-speed blender and grind until just Incorporated, and tip into an air tight jar. This will keep well in a jar for at least a month.

Rachel Martino

A great alternative to parmesan cheese, and good sprinkled liberally over salads with a balsamic vinaigrette.

Eastern emerald green salad | R | GF | V | Low GI |

SERVES 4 TO 6

- ½ an avocado
- 20g fresh mint, or a small bunch
- 30g of fresh coriander, or a small bunch
- 30g of fresh basil, or a small bunch
- 3 dates, soaked in water
- 1 tbsp olive oil
- 2 limes, juiced
- ½ cup of water
- 1 head of lettuce
- 1 large head of chicory or endive
- ½ whole cucumber
- 1 red pepper
- 1 semi-ripe pear
- Pinch of salt

Whizz together the avocado, mint, coriander, basil, dates, olive oil, lime juice, salt and water in a food processor to make the dressing. Blend together all the ingredients to make a smooth creamy dressing, adding a little more water if you need to.

Separate the chicory and lettuce leaves and put them in a large salad bowl. Cut the cucumber in half lengthways, and slice on the diagonal. Cut the red pepper into thin strips, along with the pear. When you are ready to serve, pour the green salad dressing over the salad. Use your hands to toss the salad, and finally scatter the sliced pear over the top.

Serve the salad alone or with a grain based dish such as the red pepper and freekeh pilaf on page 12.

Rachel Martino

Beetroot ravioli with pesto, 'sour cream' and fresh pomegranate seeds | R | GF | V | Low GI |

SERVES 4 AS A STARTER

- 2 raw beetroots
- 2 tbsp extra virgin olive oil
- 1 ½ lemon
- 125ml olive oil
- Large bunch of fresh basil
- 1 clove of garlic or wild garlic
- 75g cashew nuts, soaked
- 75g macadamia nuts, soaked
- 1 tsp cider vinegar
- 1 tsp probiotic powder (optional)
- 60ml water
- Handful of fresh pomegranate seeds

Soak the cashew nuts and macadamia nuts in a bowl of water, and set aside.

Peel the beetroots. Using a very sharp knife cut the beetroot into paper thin rounds, or use a mandolin if you have one.

Tip the beetroot rounds into a bowl, squeeze over the juice of half a lemon and drizzle over 2 tablespoons of extra virgin olive oil, and set aside.

Put the fresh basil leaves into a blender, along with 125ml of olive oil and the garlic, or wild garlic if you have any. Blitz together the ingredients and pour the basil oil into a small jug or glass. If you want very refined oil you can strain it, otherwise the vibrant green oil can be used as it is.

To make the 'sour cream' add the drained cashew nuts, macadamia nuts, cider vinegar, probiotic powder and water to a high speed blender. Blend together the ingredients until they are smooth and creamy, and taste for seasoning.

Using a large serving plate, lay out half of the beetroot rounds. Spoon on a small spoonful of the 'sour cream' and top with another beetroot round. When you are ready to serve, drizzle over the basil oil and scatter over fresh pomegranate seeds.

Rachel Martino

Serve with a seasonal green salad.

Vegan raw pesto

- 120g basil
- 60g pine nuts or brazil nuts
- 1 cup of extra virgin olive oil
- A good pinch of Himalayan salt
- 1 large clove garlic
- 2 tbsp nutritional yeast
- 1 pinch chipotle chilli powder
- A squeeze of lemon juice, optional

Place the nuts, salt, garlic, nutritional yeast and chipotle into a food blender and whizz together. Gradually add the olive oil and finally the basil blend together. Taste and check for seasoning. Add a dash of fresh lemon juice if need be.

Rachel Martino

Spiralizing | R | V | GF | Low GI |

Vegetables that are good for spiralizing:

- Sweet potato
- Courgette
- Butternut squash
- Potato
- Beetroot
- Carrot
- Turnip
- Kohlrabi
- Mooli
- Cucumber

It is easy to spiralize large quantities of vegetables in advance – they keep well in the fridge for a few days, especially if kept in a bowl of cold water. Some spiralized vegetables can be eaten raw, others definitely need cooking, such as potatoes. You can do this by boiling them quickly in a large pan of salted water, or by putting your vegetables into a large baking dish, seasoning with salt and pepper and a little oil, and cooking them a preheated oven – 180°C – for ten minutes, or until al dente.

Allow 150–200g of spiralized vegetable per person.

Treat your spiralized vegetables as pasta, and combine them with pesto and other traditional pasta sauces.

Courgette 'pasta' with marinated mushrooms & kale | R | V | GF | Low GI |

SERVES 4

- 4 x courgettes
- 150g cashew nuts, soaked for 4 hours and rinsed
- 2 tbsp nutritional yeast
- 1½ lemons, juiced
- 1 portobello mushroom
- 1 tsp balsamic vinegar
- 2 tbsp olive oil
- ½ tsp garlic powder
- 4 handfuls of kale, shredded into small pieces
- Sea salt
- Black pepper

Spiralize the courgettes, and set aside.

To make the cheese sauce place the cashews, nutritional yeast, and the juice of one whole lemon into a blender. Blend at a high speed to make a creamy sauce, adding enough water as necessary to achieve the desired consistency. Add sea salt and black pepper to taste.

Cut the Portobello mushroom into small cubes. Make a marinade with the balsamic vinegar, a tablespoon of olive oil, a quarter of a teaspoon of garlic powder and a pinch of salt. Massage the mushroom cubes with the marinade and leave for one hour, or until they have softened. If you have a dehydrator, you can dehydrate for a bit to soften faster.

Shred the kale in to small pieces and tip it into a large mixing bowl. Mix together one tablespoon of olive oil, one tablespoon of lemon juice, a quarter of a teaspoon of garlic powder and a pinch of salt. Massage the marinade into the kale to soften.

To serve, mix the courgette pasta with some of the cheese sauce. Add the marinated mushrooms and place on a plate surrounded by the marinated kale, topping up with some extra cream sauce.

You can also add sundried tomatoes chopped in small pieces and other veggies marinated like the kale for some extra crunch.

Nama – Artisan Raw Foods restaurant, London

Courgette 'pasta' alla marinara | R | V | GF | Low GI |

SERVES 4

- 3 medium zucchinis
- 10 large fresh tomatoes, peeled and diced
- 55g sundried tomatoes, soaked
- 1 red pepper, chopped
- ½ tsp garlic, minced
- 2 tbsp chopped onion
- 1 tbsp chopped fresh basil or 1 teaspoon dried basil
- 1 tsp coconut sugar (or other sweetener of your choice)
- 1 tbsp dried Italian herbs
- Freshly ground black pepper
- Sea salt
- Black & green olives, sliced to garnish

Spiralise the courgettes and set aside.

Blend together all the remaining ingredients, apart from the olives, and warm in the dehydrator, or over an extremely low heat in a pan. Alternatively you can serve the sauce at room temperature.

Pour the marinara sauce over your courgette pasta, garnish with sliced black and green olives and serve.

If you have extra time you could add dehydrated red peppers, courgettes and cherry tomatoes to the sauce.

Nama – Artisan Raw Foods restaurant, London

Jerusalem artichoke, parsley and hazelnut salad | R | GF | V | Low GI |

SERVES 6

- Cup olive oil
- Cup of lemon juice
- Pinch of grated nutmeg
- Sea salt and black pepper
- 6 medium Jerusalem artichokes, washed
- 50g chopped hazelnuts
- 80g flat leaf parsley, roughly chopped

Whisk together, either by hand or in a food processor, the olive oil, lemon juice, nutmeg, salt and pepper, and set the dressing aside in a jug.

Wash the artichokes, and slice into matchsticks with a sharp knife. Tip the sliced artichokes into a large salad bowl. Sprinkle over the chopped hazelnuts and the roughly chopped parsley. Pour over the salad dressing, a little at a time, and toss together the salad using your hands, adding as much dressing as you like.

Serve immediately.

Rachel Martino

Italian mushroom towers | R | GF | V | Low GI |

For this recipe it's important to buy good quality tomatoes as they will make all the difference to the flavour. Beef tomatoes are a good size.

MAKES 4–6 TOWERS

- 4 small portobello mushrooms or large chestnut mushrooms
- 2 tbsp tamari
- Pinch of dried thyme and oregano
- 3 large ripe beef tomatoes
- 2 courgettes
- Olive oil
- Sea salt
- Fresh raw vegan pesto, on page 42

Mix together the tamari and the dried herbs in a bowl.

Using a mandolin, slice the mushrooms into thin rounds. If you don't have a mandolin, use a sharp knife and cut the mushrooms as thinly as you can. Mix the mushrooms with the tamari and herbs in a container with a lid, or in a bowl with cling film, and leave to soften and marinate.

Slice the courgettes into very thin rounds and coat with a little olive oil and sea salt. Slice the tomatoes into thin rounds.

In order to assemble the towers, start with the largest tomato slices as the base, then add the courgette rounds. You will need to use a couple of courgette rounds in a single layer to cover the tomato slice if your tomatoes are very large.

Next layer the marinated mushrooms. Repeat the process, ending with a mushroom layer at the top of the stack. Using a teaspoon top with a little raw vegan basil pesto.

Stacey Gledhill

Raw cauliflower tabouleh | R | V | GF | Low GI |

SERVES 4–6

- 1 small cauliflower
- 1 small head of broccoli
- 100g pine nuts (you can toast the pine nuts if you are not 100% raw)
- 80g sultanas
- A bunch of mint, roughly chopped
- A bunch of flat leaf parsley, roughly chopped
- Juice of 1 lemon
- 4 tbsp olive oil
- Sea salt
- Black pepper
- Pomegranate seeds
- 2 finely sliced celery stalks, optional

Remove the leaves and big stalks from the cauliflower and broccoli, and cut them into chunks.

Put them into the bowl of a food processor and process briefly until they resemble couscous in texture. Don't over chop or the cauliflower and broccoli will become mushy, and it may be a good idea to process in batches to avoid any becoming pulverised.

Tip the 'couscous' into a salad bowl. Add the sultanas, pine nuts, mint, parsley, lemon juice, olive oil, salt and pepper. Taste and adjust the seasoning; you may need to add more lemon or olive oil. If you're using pomegranate seeds and finely sliced celery add them now.

You can prepare this salad in advance and let the flavours infuse if you like. It needs to be presented on a strong coloured bowl or plate to looks its best.

Sybille Pouzet

Autumn rainbow salad | R | V | GF | Low GI |

SERVES 4–6

- 2 large medjool dates
- 125ml olive oil
- 60–80ml lemon juice
- Sliver of unwaxed lemon peel
- Sea salt and black pepper
- 200g mixed salad leaves
- 1 beetroot, preferably candy beetroot, cut into matchsticks
- 1 small apple, cut into matchsticks
- 2 carrots, heirloom if possible, cut into matchsticks

To make the salad dressing put the dates, olive oil, lemon juice, sliver of lemon rind, salt and pepper in to a food processor and blend it all together, allowing it to emulsify the dressing whilst also chopping the lemon rind and dates very finely.

Peel the beetroot and cut it into matchsticks, along with the apple and the carrots. Tip the salad leaves into a large salad bowl, and add the beetroot, apple and carrot.

Just before serving pour over the dressing and toss the salad together with your hands.

Rachel Martino

Detox rainbow salad with chlorella dressing | R | V | GF | Low GI |

This salad will fill you up and give you plenty of energy for the day ahead plus the chlorella gives a protein boost. Any remaining dressing can be kept in the fridge for up to 5 days.

SERVES 4

- 300ml olive oil
- 2 tbsp fresh lemon juice
- 4 tbsp apple cider vinegar
- 3 garlic cloves, shoots removed
- 60g diced leeks
- 2 tsp chlorella powder
- 150g julienned courgettes
- 60g julienned carrots
- 60g hemp seeds (protein rich)
- 4 tbsp white sesame seeds
- 70g shaved red cabbage
- 70g shaved savoy cabbage
- 70g julienned red peppers
- 70g julienned yellow peppers
- 220g thinly sliced greens (lettuce, spinach, fresh herbs such as coriander)
- 30g diced leeks
- Sea salt to taste

To make the green dressing for the salad, blend or whisk together the olive oil, lemon juice, apple vinegar, garlic, 30g of diced leeks, chlorella powder and sea salt to taste, until all the ingredients are thoroughly mixed and incorporated. Pour the dressing into a jug and set aside.

Add the shaved and julienned vegetables to a large mixing bowl, along with the hemp seeds and sesame seeds. Add as much salad dressing as you need, mixing up the salad with your hands and allowing it to soften slightly before serving. Garnish the salad with micro herbs, seeds or crushed nuts.

Nama – Artisan Raw Foods restaurant, London

Tanya's raw carrot cakes with cream cheese icing | R | GF | V |

- 5 medium carrots, grated
- 1 cup pitted dates, soaked overnight
- 1 cup dried apricots
- 1 cup ground flaxseeds
- 1 tsp cinnamon
- 1 tsp mixed spice
- 1 tsp vanilla powder
- ½ tsp sea salt
- 1 cup cashews, soaked overnight
- 3 tbsp coconut oil
- 3 tbsp agave nectar
- Juice of 1 lemon
- 1 tsp vanilla extract
- Pinch salt

Process the grated carrots with the dates and apricots using the S blade of your food processer.

Add the flaxseeds, cinnamon, mixed spice, vanilla powder and salt, and process again until well combined.?

Form the mixture into balls and place them into mini cupcake cases. Alternatively press them into cookies. You can eat the cakes right away, or dehydrate them first at 110°F / 43°C for 8–10 hours to create a cake-like crust.

To make the cream cheese icing, blend together the soaked cashew nuts, coconut oil, agave nectar, lemon juice, vanilla extract and salt in a high speed blender, using a tamper if you have one.

Transfer the icing to the fridge to cool for an hour before spreading the over the carrot cakes.

Tanya Maher – **Tanya's Cafe, London**

Green tea ice cream | R | V | GF |

SERVES 4

- 130g cashew nuts
- 1 small avocado
- 1 ripe banana
- 1 tbsp macha green tea powder
- ¼ tsp Himalayan pink salt
- ¼ tsp vanilla powder or vanilla extract
- ¼ tsp blue green algae crystals – optional
- 210ml water
- 120ml coconut nectar (or maple syrup, although it is not 100% raw)
- 5–10 drops of SweetLeaf stevia extract – optional
- 2 tbsp coconut oil, melted gently

Add all the ingredients, except the coconut oil, into a high speed blender and process until smooth. Add the coconut oil, and blend until incorporated.

Pour the mixture into an ice cream machine and follow the normal directions. You can also make this without a machine, by pouring the mixture into a Tupperware tub, but it will need stirring a few times like any other ice cream as it freezes.

Rachel Martino

Low GI (o) if you use coconut nectar.
Remove the ice cream from the freezer a good ten minutes before serving to let it soften. This ice cream is best eaten the day that it is made. For an indulgent touch, serve it with chocolate cardamom sauce on page 58.

Raw chocolate brownie with ganache icing | R | V | GF |

MAKES APPROXIMATELY 15 SMALL SQUARES

- 100g pecan nuts
- 150g cashew nuts
- 100g cacao powder
- 200g dates + about 60ml water (more or less depending on the dryness of your dates)
- 1 tsp raw vanilla extract
- 140ml agave syrup
- 100g coconut oil
- 35g cacao powder
- 70ml agave syrup
- Sea salt

Put the cashew and pecan nuts in a food processor and process until crumbly, and then transfer to a large bowl. Add the cacao powder and a pinch of salt, and mix thoroughly with a large spoon.

Place the dates in to the food processor, and blend with a little water to make a date paste. Be careful not to add too much water, otherwise the brownie will be wet. Add the vanilla and 70ml of the agave syrup, and blend well.

Add the date paste to the dry ingredients and mix well, which will take some muscle as it is a stiff mixture. Press the mixture firmly into a shallow square or rectangular brownie pan, approximately 20cm × 30cm in size. You may find it beneficial to line the pan with baking parchment.

To make the ganache icing, melt the coconut oil in a bain-marie.

Once it is melted, slowly add the cacao powder, whisking constantly. Add 70ml of agave syrup and sea salt, and stir well.

Pour the ganache over the brownie so that it covers it well, and let it firm up in the fridge until set, which should take about one hour. When it is firm remove it from the fridge and cut into squares. These brownies are very rich, so make sure that you cut them into small-ish squares.

Sybille Pouzet

Raw chocolate torte | R | V | GF |

- 150g almonds or coconut chips, or a mix of both
- 160g raisins (or chopped up figs) or any dried fruit
- 3 tbsp coconut oil melted
- 3 tsp vanilla extract
- 2 tsp cinnamon
- Sea salt
- 1–2 avocados
- 70g raw cacao powder
- 40g coconut oil (melted)
- 70g coconut sugar
- 175ml of almond milk
- 50g coconut cream (melted)

Blend together the almonds, raisins or dried fruit, 3 tablespoons of coconut oil, 3 teaspoons of vanilla extract, the cinnamon and a healthy pinch of salt in a high speed food processor. When the ingredients are combined and press into a spring form cake tin, and place it in the fridge to set.

Peel the avocados, remove the stones and add the flesh to a high speed blender. Blend them until smooth, then add the cacao powder, 40g of coconut oil, coconut sugar, almond milk and coconut cream. Pour the mixture over the base and leave it to set in the fridge.

Decorate with fresh berries or cacao nibs before serving.

Wild Food Café, London

Keep this incredibly decandent desert in the fridge until you are ready to eat it. It keeps well for a good 3 days in the fridge.

Chocolate cardamom sauce | R | V | GF |

MAKES 1 SMALL JAR

- 45g of raw cocoa powder
- 125ml of maple syrup
- ¼ tsp ground cardamom
- 1 pinch of sea salt
- ¼ tsp vanilla extract
- 1 tbsp coconut oil, melted

Put all of the ingredients into a food processor, and blend together until completely smooth.

Transfer the sauce to a jar, and keep in the fridge until needed. It can be warmed through in a dehydrator or on a very low heat on the hob.

Serve it with the green tea ice cream on page 54, or if you are not 100% raw, try it with good quality vanilla ice cream. Alternatively this sauce can be enjoyed dribbled over the raw chocolate torte on page 56.

Rachel Martino

Raw chocolates | R | V | GF |

- 70g raw cacao butter
- 6 tbsp raw cacao powder
- 3 tbsp agave syrup / date syrup/ coconut nectar / maple syrup

Break the cacao butter into small pieces, or whizz it up in the magimix. Empty it into a bowl and melt it gently over a bain-marie, ensuring that the temperature does not rise above 40°C.

When it is melted stir in the cocao powder and the agave syrup. Using a balloon whisk give it a good stir, ensuring the powder is properly incorporated.

Add a pinch of sea salt, tangerine zest or hazelnuts if you so wish.

Spoon into a mould and put in the fridge to set for at least 20 minutes.

Annabel Graham-Wood

As this chocolate is untempered it is not as stable as normal chocolate and can melt more rapidly when out of the fridge.
You can set this chocolate in a silicone mould, and store in a cool cupboard or the fridge.

Vegan food

Vegan food

The vegan diet is one which showcases plant-based foods. The term vegan describes a diet and lifestyle which excludes the use of all animal bi-products. In its strictest form, products such as meat, fish, eggs, dairy, honey and leather are all excluded from your diet and life.

From a culinary perspective, it's important to keep in mind that both the food and also the process are animal free. For instance some food colourings and additives, although thought to be animal free, may be derived from animal sources (ie. gelatine).

In this chapter we explore some delicious vegan recipes. You don't have to be living a vegan lifestyle to enjoy these delicious recipes, so feel free to try them on their own, or paired with any other dishes in the book.

Babaganoush | V | GF option – without pitta bread | Low GI |

SERVES 4 AS A DIP OR SIDE DISH

- 3 aubergines
- ½ clove of garlic, crushed
- 3 tbsp tahini
- 2 tbsp olive oil
- Juice of 1 lemon
- Sea salt and black pepper

Preheat the grill to its maximum heat.

Using a sharp knife, slice the stalk end off the aubergines and keep them whole. Prick each aubergine all over to stop them exploding, and place them under the grill. Grill the aubergines until their skins go crisp and wrinkly, and then turn them over in order to cook the other side.

Once they are blackened all over and the flesh inside is soft, place them into a bowl and allow them to rest a while.

When the aubergines are cool enough to handle, scrape the soft flesh and juices into a bowl. Add the crushed garlic, the tahini, lemon juice and olive oil. Using a balloon or electric whisk, bring together the babaganoush, whisking enough to create a creaminess, but leaving a lumpy texture.

Check the seasoning and add salt and pepper if needed, or more lemon juice.

Serve with warm pitta breads and a pulse based salad. Warm dry toasted walnuts are a delicious accompaniment, and a good source of protein.

Mexican black bean soup | GF | GF | Low GI |

SERVES 4

- 2 tins of black beans, drained and rinsed
- 2 tbsp coconut oil
- 1 onion, finely diced
- 4 cloves garlic, crushed
- 1 tbsp ground cumin
- 2–3 tsp chipotle powder, or crushed chipotle chillis
- 1 litre vegetable stock, approximately
- 50g coconut cream
- 1–2 limes, juiced
- Small bunch coriander chopped

Add the coconut oil to a medium saucepan, add the chopped onion and cook on a low heat for around 10 minutes until very soft. Stir in the garlic and cook for another few minutes, and then stir in the spices, followed by the black beans.

Cover the beans with just half of the stock, so that the beans are just covered. It should still be quite thick as you can always add more later to get it to the consistency you want. Simmer the soup for 20 minutes on a low heat to bring the flavours together, stirring occasionally.

Remove half of the soup from the pan. Blend half of the soup until smooth and then add it back to the pan with the unblended half. Add the lime juice to taste, stir in the coconut cream and add more chipotle if you like some extra heat. If the soup is too thick, add some more stock to thin in down. Season with salt if you need to.

Divide the soup into bowls and garnish with a little coriander, and serve.

You can serve this with a spoon of guacamole.

Kali Hamm

Grilled bittersweet salad with toasted pecans and sherry vinegar dressing | V | GF | Low GI |

SERVES 4

- 1 head of radicchio
- 1 fennel
- 1 large chicory or 2 small
- 1 tbsp olive oil
- 90g wild rocket
- 1 bunch of tarragon leaves
- 1 bunch of dill leaves
- 1 bunch of mint leaves
- 100g pecans, toasted and roughly chopped
- ½ tsp cayenne pepper
- 1 tsp maple syrup or date syrup
- 1 tbsp sherry vinegar
- ½ clove of crushed garlic – optional
- 1 ripe pear, cut into thin slices
- 3 tbsp olive oil
- Sea salt and fresh black pepper

Slice the radicchio in half, cut out the tough middle and then cut each half into three. Do the same for the chicory, and cut the fennel into eighths. Toss them separately in a drizzle of olive oil and season with salt and pepper.

Heat a griddle pan, or a heavy bottomed frying pan, on a high heat until smoking hot. Griddle the vegetables separately, making sure you don't over crowd the pan. They should have dark grill marks and will take on that great grilled flavour, but do not over cook them as you want them to maintain some crunch.

Transfer the veg to a large salad bowl when they are done. Toast the pecan nuts in a dry frying pan, roughly break them up with a rolling pin and transfer them to the salad bowl.

To make the dressing, whisk together the cayenne pepper, maple/date syrup, sherry vinegar and olive oil, adding garlic if you wish.

Dress the griddled chicory, fennel, radicchio and pecans quickly with your hands. Add the rocket, and the tarragon, mint and dill leaves and sliced pear, and quickly mix everything together using your hands again.

Serve immediately.

This is perfect as a side salad, or can be made into a more filling meal by adding a pulse, or serving with a risotto.

Kali Hamm

Red camargue rice salad with peppers and parsley | V | GF | Low GI |

SERVES 4

- 300g of Camargue Red rice
- Gluten free vegetable stock cube
- 5 tbsp olive oil
- 3 red bell peppers
- 4 vine tomatoes
- 1 clove garlic
- 1 red onion
- Zest of ½ lemon
- Juice of 1 lemon
- Large bunch of flat leaf parsley
- Sea salt
- Black pepper
- Pre-heat the oven to 180°C.

Rinse the rice in a sieve and place into a medium sized saucepan. Cover well with fresh water, add a stock cube to the water, and bring the pan to the boil. Once the water is boiling reduce the heat, and allow the rice to simmer for approximately 30 minutes, or until cooked. This rice should have a firm texture, but not be hard.

While the rice is cooking, cut the tomatoes in half. Place the tomatoes, cut side up, into an oven tray. Peel and thinly slice the clove of garlic, and place a slice of garlic on to each tomato half. Season with salt and pepper. Half the peppers, scrape out the seeds, and cut them into rough thick strips. Transfer the peppers into the same oven pan, covering generously with around 3 tablespoons of olive oil, turning the peppers well with your handsl to ensure that they are well coated. Season well and place in the oven to cook for 25 minutes, or until the peppers and tomatoes are soft and melting, but not charred.

Dice the red onion. Heat a tablespoon of olive oil in a heavy bottomed pan, add the onion and allow it to saute until soft, and set aside.

When the rice, peppers, tomatoes and onions are cooked, remove the baked tomatoes and set aside on a plate. Combine all the ingredients in a large mixing bowl. Add the lemon zest, lemon juice, flat leaf parsley and, using a large metal spoon, mix everything together thoroughly without breaking up the peppers. Add a tablespoon of olive oil and salt and pepper if necessary.

Just before serving place the tomatoes on the top of the salad.

Hattie Deards

This is great served with the babaganoush on page 64.

Kale and french bean salad with hazelnuts and orange and ginger dressing | V | Low GI |

SERVES 6

- 2 tbsp light rapeseed oil
- ½ red chilli, finely chopped
- 2cm piece of ginger, peeled and grated
- 360g of curly kale
- 200g bag of green beans, trimmed
- 1 tbsp of extra virgin olive oil
- 1½ tbsp light soy sauce
- 1 tbsp mirin rice wine
- 1 orange, juice and zest of the whole orange
- 60 g of toasted hazelnuts
- Sea salt

Heat the oil in a frying pan or wok, add the chilli and ginger and simmer for a few minutes. Take off the heat and leave to cool.

Blanch the green beans for 2 minutes in salted boiling water, drain and plunge into a bowl of iced water. Wash the kale leaves and tear into salad sized chunks, leaving aside the stalks, and place in a large bowl. Massage the olive oil and a good sprinkle of sea salt into the leaves for a few minutes until the kale has softened and absorbed the oil. Add the green beans to the bowl when they are cool.

Add the soy sauce, mirin rice wine, orange zest and juice to the infused oil, and mix all together. When you are ready to serve the salad, pour the dressing over the kale and beans, and toss well, using your hands.

Toast the hazelnuts in a dry pan. Break them up roughly with the end of a rolling pin, and scatter over salad before serving.

Alice Dewey

GF (o) – if you use tamari instead of soy sauce.

Veggie pad thai

SERVES: 4

- 200g medium rice noodles
- 3 tbsp sunflower or light oil
- Half a bunch of spring onions, peeled and finely sliced
- 300g Chinese beansprout
- 150g golden marinated tofu
- 2 large cloves of garlic, peeled and crushed
- 2 limes
- 1 tbsp tamari soy sauce
- 1 tbsp sweet chilli sauce
- 75g shelled, unsalted, roast peanut, roughly chopped
- 2–3 tsp sesame oil
- 3 heaped tbsp. chopped coriander, plus a few extra coriander leaves

Drop the noodles into a large pan of boiling water with a little oil added. Bring the water back to the boil and cook the noodles for a minute, then drain and rinse under cold running water.

Heat a wok or large frying pan, add the oil, the spring onions and beansprouts and stir fry for a couple of minutes. Add the tofu, cook for a further minute then add the crushed ginger, the juice of 1 lime, the soy sauce and the chilli sauce and stir well.

Turn the heat right down and tip in the noodles. Using a serving spoon and fork, toss together all the ingredients. Add the chopped peanuts, sesame oil and coriander and toss again.

Serve the noodles in warm bowls with a few extra coriander leaves sprinkled on top. Serve with a lime wedge on the side, and put out the soy sauce, sesame oil and sweet chilli sauce so that everyone can add more if they wish.

Fiona Beckett
Beyond Baked Beans Green
Absolute Press 2004

Herby butter bean stew | V | GF | Low GI |

SERVES 6

- 4 tbsp olive oil
- 1 onion, thinly sliced
- 2 stalks of fresh rosemary, leaves removed and roughly chopped
- 2 leeks, thinly sliced
- 4 cloves garlic, thinly sliced
- 2 tsp dried sage
- 4 tins of butter beans (drained weight 940g)
- 3 stalks of lemon thyme, leaves removed
- 400ml vegetable stock
- 1 lemon, juiced
- Sea salt and black pepper

Heat the olive oil in a large heavy bottomed pan. Saute the onion, and add the chopped rosemary. Cook for 2 or 3 minutes on a medium heat.

Add the leeks and garlic, and add 2 teaspoons of dried sage. Stir well and add the drained butter beans and the lemon thyme leaves. Pour over 400ml of vegetable stock, and leave the stew to simmer for 20 to 25 minutes.

When you are ready to eat, season the stew well with salt and pepper, lemon juice and stir in whole basil leaves.

Blues

Great eaten with a chunk of fresh crusty bread, or made into more of a meal with some grilled halibut and a salsa verde.

Chickpea, tamarind and cinnamon curry | V | GF | Low GI |

SERVES 6

- 100g desiccated coconut
- 2 tsp coriander seeds, or ground coriander
- 8 curry leaves
- 2 cloves of garlic, finely sliced
- 2 dried birds eye chillis
- 4 tbsp vegetable oil
- 1 cinnamon stick
- 1 onion, cut into medium sized cubes
- 1 tsp turmeric powder
- 1 tsp mild chilli powder
- 3 vine tomatoes, cut into eighths
- 2 tins of chickpeas, 240g drained weight each
- 3 tbsp tamarind water (made from 1 tbsp of tamarind pulp)
- 1 lime, juiced
- 200ml coconut milk
- 2 tsp black mustard seeds
- Handful of fresh chopped coriander

If you are using tamarind paste or pulp, place 1 tablespoon of it into a small bowl. Add 3 tablespoons of water and mix well, allowing it to dissolve and create the tamarind water. If you are using fresh tamarind pulp you may need to strain the tamarind liquid before using it. Set it aside.

Make the masala first before making the curry. Toast the coconut, coriander seeds or ground coriander, curry leaves, garlic and chillis together in a dry frying pan for a few minutes. Do this on a gentle heat, as you don't want the coconut to burn. Transfer the mixture to a blender or grinder, add 250ml of water, and blend to as much of a paste as possible, which can take a few minutes.

In a wide and deep frying pan, or a large saucepan, heat 3 tablespoons of the vegetable oil. Add the onions and cinnamon stick. Sprinkle over a little salt and cook for five minutes, or until the onion start to soften and turn transparent. Add the turmeric and chilli powder, stir well and then add the tomatoes and chickpeas.

Add the masala paste to the curry, and cook on a low heat for ten minutes, stirring occasionally to make sure that it doesn't stick to the bottom of the pan. Add the coconut milk and the tamarind water, and stir thoroughly. Turn the heat right down and allow it to gently bubble for a further 5 minutes.

In a small frying pan heat the remaining tablespoon of oil. Add the mustard seeds and heat until the mustard seeds begin to pop. Pour the mixture into the curry, stir and remove from the heat. Scatter over some freshly chopped coriander.

Serve with brown rice and a good spoonful of mango chutney.

Hattie Deards

Make this curry in advance if you want to, and
serve with brown rice or cauliflower rice on page 74.

Cauliflower rice | V | GF | Low GI |

- 1 cauliflower
- 1 large firm/unripe mango
- 1 bunch of mint
- 100g cashew nuts
- Salt and pepper

Remove the outer leaves and the core of the cauliflower, and break it into small florets.

Tip the florets into a food processor, and, using the S-blade, pulse the cauliflower until it resembles cous-cous or rice, making sure you do not over blend it. Tip the cauliflower rice into a large mixing bowl.

Peel the mango and cut it into fine dice, and add it to the cauliflower.

Toast the cashew nuts in a dry frying pan and add it to the bowl, along with the roughly chopped mint. Add a good crunch of sea salt and mix all the ingredients together thoroughly.

Serve with any curry of your choice.

Bridget Gladwin

Firey beetroot jam | V | GF |

MAKES 2 LARGE JARS

- 5 red peppers deseeded & roughly chopped
- 4 red chillies, seeds removed
- 3 garlic cloves peeled
- 50g peeled ginger
- 500g raw beetroot
- 2 dried birds eye chillis
- 200g muscovado sugar
- 175ml cider vinegar
- 1 tsp fennel seeds
- 1 tsp mustard seeds
- 1 tsp caraway seeds

Blend together the peppers, chillies, garlic, stem ginger and beetroot in a food processor.

Pour in to a heavy based pan with the sugars, vinegar and seeds and bring to the boil.

Remove any scum from the surface and cook until thick, sticky and bubbling, about 40–60 minutes.

Leave for 10 minutes then pour in to sterilised jars. When completely cold store in the fridge.

Makes approximately 2 to 3 jars.

Lydia France

Keep this jam to serve with smoked fish, cold meat and cheese.

Blueberry cheesecake with a vanilla spice crumbly base | R | V | GF |

SERVES 6–8

- 350g cashew nuts
- 70g brazil nuts
- ¼ tsp sea salt or Himalayan salt
- ¼ tsp vanilla powder or 1 tsp vanilla extract
- 1 tbsp coconut sugar
- 100g chopped dates
- 1 pinch cinnamon
- Juice and zest of 1 large orange
- 70ml agave syrup or maple syrup
- 70ml coconut oil
- Juice of ½ a lemon
- Pinch of sea salt
- 500g fresh blueberries

To make the crumbly base, add 150g of the cashew nuts, the brazil nuts, salt, vanilla and coconut sugar to a food processor and whizz together until you have a crumbly texture. Add the dates and cinnamon and continue to process until everything is combined.

Press the base into a 20–23cm non-stick spring form – or loose base – cake tin. Place the tin in the fridge to firm up for at least an hour.

To make the blueberry topping, process together 200g of cashew nuts, the juice and zest of one large orange, the agave/maple syrup, coconut oil, lemon juice, salt and blueberries. This is best done in a high speed processor as you want to get the mixture as smooth as possible, so that it resembles a creamy batter.

Poor the blueberry mixture over the base and return your cheesecake to the fridge for at least 90 minutes to set. When you are ready to serve, scatter over some fresh blueberries, or any berries of your choice.

Rachel Martino and Sarah Willes

If you do not want a full cheesecake, you can serve the base with a berry compote and some good quality ice cream.
Alternatively, use the base mixture to make your own chocolates. Hand roll the nutty base into small balls, dip them into chocolate that has been melted over a bain marie, and refridgerate to set.

Hazelnut and coffee ice cream | V | GF |

- 4 medium ripe bananas, peeled
- 500g carton of coconut cream
- 5 tbsp strong espresso coffee
- 100g whole hazelnuts, skin on

Preheat the oven to 180°C.

Using a large knife roughly chop the hazelnuts on a board, and tip them onto a baking tray. Toast the nuts in the oven for 5 to 10 minutes, depending on their size, until just golden.

Make a strong espresso coffee and set aside.

Peel the bananas and add them to a blender. Add the coconut cream, and spoon in five tablespoons of espresso coffee. Blend everything together until completely smooth.

Lightly toast the chopped hazlenuts and mix into the ice cream mixture. Pour the mix into an ice cream maker and follow manufacturers instructions. If you do not have one, you can make this ice cream without one, by pouring the mixture into a large Tupperware box or mixing bowl, and stir intermittently while it freezes.

You can sweeten this ice cream with a little coconut nectar or maple syrup, or add a squeeze of lime if needed.

Sarah Willes

Make sure you eat this ice cream on the day that you make it, as it does not keep well in the freezer.

Rachel's refreshers | R | Low GI | GF |

The quality of juices are going to vary wildly depending on the juicer they go through. The following juices have always worked well in a twin gear juicer, but may be very different if made with a centrifugal style juicer. Modify all the ingredients for your own tastes …

Indian summer green

- 1 bunch of mint
- 5 large leaves of romaine lettuce
- ¼ – ½ gaia melon
- ½ courgette
- ½ lemon, peeled
- ½ cucumber

Middle Eastern Beet

- 1 golden beetroot
- 1 pomegranate
- 2 cucumbers
- 1 bunch of mint

Golden Beet

- 2–3 pears
- 1 small golden beetroot
- Large handful of parsley

Summer Green

- ¼ pineapple
- 1 cucumber
- 1 bunch of mint

Dark Beet

- 1 red beet
- 1 orange, peeled
- ½ an apple
- 2–3 stalks of celery
- 2 generous handfuls of greens, mixed winter salad, spinach or chard
- ½ cucumber

Spicy Pear

- 2 pears
- 4 leaves of chard
- ½ lemon, peeled
- 2 slices of root ginger

Asian green

- ⅓ pineapple
- 10 leaves of spinach
- Small handful of basil
- Small handful of coriander
- Sprig of mint
- 1 lime, peeled
- ½ cucumber
- Slice of root ginger

Sweet & spicy carrot

- 3 large carrots
- 1 pear
- 1 apple
- ½ lemon, peeled
- Small knob of peeled root ginger
- Sprinkle of cinnamon at the end

Jetlag pick-me-up | R | V | GF |

- 1 cucumber
- 2 apples
- Small handful of mint leaves

Wash the cucumber and apples, and cut into the chunks that are the right size for your juicer.

Juice everything along with the mint leaves. Serve this extremely refreshing drink immediately with ice cubes, as it will start to oxidize and turn brown if left for any length of time.

Sarah Willes

This is good after a long flight. It's refreshing and rehydrating, and is a natural pick-me-up.

City smoothie | R | Low GI | GF |

- 500ml hibiscus or rosehip tea, infused and cooled
- 250g frozen berries
- 1 avocado, peeled and stone removed
- 1 handful of washed kale leaves, stems removed
- 2 tsp chia seeds
- 2 tsp ground cinnamon
- 1 tbsp raw honey, or 4 drops of sweet leaf stevia

Soak the chia seeds in half a cup of water for approximately 15 minutes.

Add all the ingredients to a high speed blender, and blend for 30 to 60 seconds or until fully incorporated and smooth. Alternatively add half the tea to the blender along with the other ingredients, blend for 30 to 60 seconds, and then add the remaining tea and continue to blend.

Serve well chilled.

Rachel Martino

V (o) – use stevia instead of honey.
Transfer the smoothie to a flask to have as a great breakfast or snack when you are on-the-go.

Low glycaemic food

Low glycaemic food

A low glycaemic diet is one that selects foods on the basis of minimal alteration of circulating glucose levels, and it is especially helpful for people who are diabetic.

Low Glycaemic Index (GI) and low Glycaemic Load (GL) are related, but are not the same. So what's the difference?

The glycaemic index is a measure of the level of carbohydrate of a given food. Glycaemic Load on the other hand, estimates the affect food will have on one's blood sugar levels. GL is based on GI, but also takes into account the serving size of any given food or meal.

In this chapter we present a variety of recipes designed with a low glycaemic impact in mind. We have considered both GI and GL. Although we are presenting recipes designed with blood sugar management in mind, please feel free to modify these recipes to suit those who will enjoy them. If you're catering for someone requiring a particularly low intake of sugar, such as those who are diabetic, please use the natural sweetener chart for the best substitution. For example, some sweeteners are used in the recipes with a low – moderate glycaemic load and you may prefer to substitute a lower one (indicated with * on the sugars chart on page X or eliminate the sweetener all together instead.

Kohlrabi with ricotta and pears | GF | Low GI |

SERVES 4

- 1 large kohlrabi
- 2 fresh ripe pears
- 190g ricotta cheese
- 1 lemon
- Olive oil
- Small bunch of fresh mint
- Sea salt and black pepper

Peel, half and core the pears, and slice thinly. Arrange the pears on a plate and squeeze over the juice of half a lemon to prevent them from browning.

Peel and slice the kohlrabi as thinly as you can. Scatter the kohlrabi over the pears, and, using a teaspoon, spoon over scoops of ricotta. Grate over the zest of half a lemon, then squeeze over the juice of the whole lemon, and scatter over the mint.

Season with salt and pepper, and dress with olive oil.

Serve with warm walnut bread as a starter.

If you are unable to find kohlrabi, you can use fennel instead.

Sarah Willes

Carrot, red cabbage, orange, almond and watercress salad | Low GI | GF |

SERVES 6

- 6 tbsp rapeseed oil
- 1 red cabbage, thinly shredded
- 2 tsp ground all spice
- 60ml red wine vinegar
- 2 tbsp brown sugar
- 4 yellow carrots, peeled and thinly sliced into matchsticks
- 4 purple carrots, peeled and thinly sliced into matchsticks
- 2 tsp caraway seeds
- 150g whole blanched almonds
- 2 tsp honey
- 2 oranges, blood orange if possible
- 1 lemon, juiced
- Sea salt and black pepper
- Hairy bittercress or watercress

Thinly shred the red cabbage with a sharp knife. Add 2 tablespoons of rapeseed oil to a large heavy bottomed pan, and add the red cabbage. Add the ground all spice, the red wine vinegar and the brown sugar, and stir well. Season the cabbage with salt and pepper, add a lid and allow it to soften for around 45 minutes. Set it aside to cool if you have enough time.

Meanwhile peel the carrots, cut into batons and add to a bowl. Add 2 teaspoons of caraway seeds, 2 tablespoons of rapeseed oil and season well with salt and pepper. Using your hands stir up the carrots, ensuring that they are all well covered with oil and seasoning.

Heat a griddle pan or a large frying pan on the hob. Add the carrots and allow them to char slightly, tossing and moving them regularly. Take note that the purple carrots will take slightly longer to cook than the lighter coloured ones. They should still have some crunch, but be charred in places. When done, tip the carrots on to a plate to cool.

Add 2 teaspoons of honey to a dry frying pan, along with 2 tablespoons of rapeseed oil, some salt and some pepper. Heat the pan and add the almonds. Allow the almonds to bubble in the mixture, and stir continually. Remove when they are golden and set aside.

Using a sharp knife peel the oranges, removing all the pith. Cut the orange into segments and set aside.

Assemble the salad in a large salad bowl or earthenware dish. Tip in the cabbage and add the carrots. Using your hands gently toss the vegetables together. Add the orange segments and half of the caramelised almonds, and again toss it all together with your hands. Squeeze over the juice of one whole lemon and stir well. Taste the salad and add more lemon, or salt and pepper, if need be.

Add the remaining caramelised almonds, and the bittercress or watercress. Quickly toss it all together and serve straight away.

Olly Gladwin

V (o) – replace honey with coconut nectar or maple syrup.

Olly Gladwin is co-owner of The Shed restaurant and Rabbit restaurant.

Lamb chops with cumin and dill tsatziki | GF | Low GI |

SERVES 6

- 12 lamb chops, preferably side loin (the chops with the rib loin)
- Extra virgin olive oil
- 3 tbsp cumin seeds, toasted and ground
- Roasted cherry tomatoes on the vine – allowing 4 per person
- 1 crisp cucumber, peeled and cut into dice
- 1 garlic clove, crushed
- Juice of 1 lemon
- 425ml Greek yoghurt or natural yoghurt
- 4 tbsp cream, optional
- 2 tbsp chopped dill
- Sea salt and freshly ground black pepper

Trim any excess fat off the chops, and lay the chops out in a single layer on a tray or plate. Brush with olive oil and season with the ground cumin seeds and pepper. Leave it to sit for at least 15 minutes, but a whole hour if possible.

If you have time, put the cucumber dice into a sieve, sprinkle with salt and allow it to drain for about 15 minutes, removing any excess moisture. Tip the cucumber into a bowl, and mix with the garlic, a dash of lemon juice, the yoghurt and the cream (if you want it extra creamy). Stir in the dill, taste and season as required.

Heat the griddle pan, season the chops with sea salt and cook in batches for a few minutes each side until crisp on the outside, but slightly pink and juicy on the inside, and the fat is crisp.

Serve 2 chops per person, with a little bowl or spoonful of tzatsiki on each plate and a branch of roasted cherry tomatoes.

Darina Allen
Easy Entertaining
Kyle Cathie 2005

Pepper cod | GF | Low GI |

SERVES 4

- 4 pieces of cod or any very fresh white fish
- 2 red romano peppers
- 1 red onion, finely chopped
- 2 tbsp light olive oil
- 1 small bunch thyme
- 2 lemons
- 300g ready cooked black beluga lentils
- 1 lemon
- 1 large clove of garlic, crushed

Pre-heat the oven to 200°C.

Grill the red pepper until its skin is blistered, and place it into a plastic bag for a while, until you are able to peel off the skin and remove the seeds. Slice them into strips and set aside.

Place the fish onto an oiled baking tray, season with salt and pepper, and the juice of one lemon. Bake the fish in the oven for 10 to 15 minutes.

While the fish is cooking, finely chop the red onion. Heat the olive oil in a deep frying pan or saucepan. Gently cook the onion for 2 minutes. Add the thyme, the rind and juice of one lemon, the crushed garlic and cook for a further 5 minutes. Stir in the lentils, season with salt and pepper, and gently heat through.

When you are ready to serve you can plate this up individually. Spoon on the lentils, then place the fish on top, and finally spoon the peppers on to the top. Serve with a large wedge of lemon.

Sarah Willes

Pim's tuna ceviche | GF | Low GI |

SERVES 4–6

- 800g fresh tuna, preferably the belly
- 1 granny smith apple
- 2 limes
- 1½ tbsp small capers
- 1 green chilli, put in the freezer in advance
- Olive oil
- Sea salt and black pepper

Keep the tuna in the fridge and prepare this dish just before you eat it, as it needs to be served as cold as possible.

Cut the tuna into cubes. Cut the apple into fine matchsticks, including the skin. Finely grate the zest of the limes and squeeze the juice, and add to the apple, tuna and capers in a large bowl.

Stir together the ingredients, and heap up the mixture on to individual plates, drizzle with olive oil and season with a little salt and black pepper. Grate over the frozen green chilli and serve immediately.

Pim Philips

There should be enough ceviche here to serve it as a main course.

Goan style mussels, pollock or monkfish | GF | Low GI |

This recipe can be prepared well in advance, or even the day before. The mussels can be replaced with clams, shrimp, or monkfish. A combination of fish and shellfish may be used, as can salmon and mackerel.

Plain rice can be served with this dish, or just crusty bread to mop up the delicious broth.

SERVES 4–6

- 2.5cm piece of fresh ginger, peeled and chopped
- 8 cloves of peeled garlic
- 110ml of water
- 4 tbsp vegetable oil
- 200g onion, peeled and sliced into semi circles
- 1–2 fresh chillis, sliced into fine rounds
- ½ tsp turmeric
- 2 tsp ground cumin
- 1½ tins (600ml) of coconut milk
- Salt
- Fresh coriander leaves

Wash the mussels, removing any loose beards. Put the ginger, garlic and water into a blender and blend to a smooth puree.

Heat the oil in a large pan and add the onions. Cook the onions until translucent. Add the ginger and garlic puree, along with the chillis, turmeric and cumin. Stir and cook for a minute. Add the coconut milk and a pinch of salt, and bring to the boil. This broth can now be put aside for when you are ready to eat.

When you are ready to serve the dish, put the mussels into the pan with the broth. Cover and place on a moderate heat and allow it to come to a gentle boil. Shake the pan occasionally, and cook for approximately 6 minutes. Check to see that all the mussels have opened, and serve immediately with fresh coriander.

If you are using monkfish or any other fish instead of mussels, bring the broth to a gentle boil. Cut the fish into 5cm pieces, and add it to the broth. Cover and simmer gently for approximately 5 minutes, or until the fish is just cooked. Serve in deeps bowls garnished with coriander leaves.

Ballymaloe Cookery School

Keralan white fish and prawn curry | GF | Low GI |

SERVES 4–6

- 1 large onion
- 800g of a mix of firm white fish and raw king prawns
- 2 tsp ground turmeric
- 1 tbsp vegetable oil
- 1 red chilli, more if you like your curry to be hot
- 5cm piece of ginger, peeled
- 1 tsp ground cumin
- 1 x 400ml tin of coconut milk
- 3 tbsp tamarind paste
- 500ml of fish stock, from concentrate
- coriander
- Sea salt

Peel the onions, cut them in half and slice them finely into half moons. Cut the white fish into large bite sized chunks and add them to a mixing bowl along with the raw prawns. Sprinkle over a little sea salt and one teaspoon of turmeric, and using your hands mix together well, and set aside.

Heat the vegetable oil in a large shallow pan or wok. Add the onions and a little salt, and cook until they have softened, stirring to stop them from sticking.

Cut the red chilli into thin slices, leaving in the seeds if you like your curry to have a little more heat. Peel the garlic and cut into thin matchstick. Add the chilli and ginger to the pan, along with the remaining turmeric and the cumin. Fry the spices with the onions for a few minutes and add the coconut milk along with the tamarind.

Boil a kettle and add the fish stock concentrate to a measuring jug. Fill the jug with 500ml of boiling water, and stir the stock to dissolve it. Pour the stock into the pan, and stir everything together well, making sure that the coconut milk is well integrated.

When you are ready to eat, add the prawns and fish to the hot curry sauce and gently simmer for a few minutes until just cooked through.

Scatter over some fresh coriander leaves.

Blues

Serve with brown rice, or cauliflower rice on page 74.

Spicy fish stew

- 3 tbsp olive oil
- 1 onion, sliced
- 1 red pepper, sliced
- 1 bulb of fennel, thinly sliced
- 200g chorizo, cut into 1cm cubes
- 200g salmon, roughly cubed
- 200g monkfish, roughly cubed
- 1 large handful of large uncooked prawns, shells on
- 1 red chilli, finely grated
- 1 large handful of mussels, cleaned
- 800g chopped fresh tomatoes or 2 tins of chopped tomatoes
- 3 cloves of garlic, finely chopped
- Pinch of nutmeg
- Pinch of cinnamon
- Pinch of sugar
- Sea salt and black pepper
- Fresh flat leaf parsley, roughly chopped

Thinly slice the onion, red pepper and fennel. Heat the olive oil in a large thick bottomed pan, and cook them slowly until starting to soften before removing them from the pan and setting them aside.

Add the chorizo and let it brown for a few minutes. Remove it from the pan and set it aside with the vegetables. Add the cubed salmon and monkfish, followed by the prawns. Cook for a further 2 minutes, then add back the vegetables, chorizo, chilli, mussels, tomatoes, finely chopped garlic, nutmeg, cinnamon and sugar. Simmer the stew for a further 15 minutes, adding a little vegetable stock if you think that it needs more liquid, and season with salt and pepper.

Ensure that the mussels are cooked through and that all are opened. Sprinkle over some roughly chopped fresh parsley, and serve in soup bowls with a wedge of fresh wholemeal bread or on its own.

James Nathan

Low GI (o) if you use a sugar substitute.
GF – ensure that the chorizo is gluten free.

Red quinoa, avocado & caramelised seeds | GF | Low GI | V |

SERVES 4

- 230g red or mixed colour quinoa
- 1 avocado, diced
- 300g fresh peas (podded)
- 300g broad beans, double podded if you have time
- 1 lemon, juiced
- 50g pumpkin seeds
- 50g sunflower seeds
- 1 tbsp balsamic vinegar
- 2 tbsp olive oil
- 1 bunch of chervil or flat leaf parsley
- Sea salt
- Black pepper

Place the quinoa in a pan with two large cups of water. Bring it to the boil, then let it simmer for ten minutes. Turn the heat off, cover the pan and set aside until all the water has been absorbed. Once cooked, let the grains cool down, and fluff with a fork if you need to and transfer to a large salad bowl.

In a saucepan of well salted boiling water, blanch the broad beans for 3 minutes and the peas for 1 minute, and then run them under cold water. If you have the time, double pod the broad beans – they are more tender and a vibrant green without their shell.

Add the seeds to a heavy bottomed frying pan. Season them well with sea salt, add the balsamic vinegar and stir well. Toast the seeds until they are just turning brown, and tip on to a plate to cool.

Mix the quinoa with the peas, broad beans, roughly chopped chervil / parsley, lemon juice, the seeds, diced avocado and olive oil. Season well with salt and pepper, and add more lemon if you need to. Serve immediately.

Sybille Pouzet

Fabulous served with the autumn rainbow salad on page 50.

Bulghur wheat with tomatoes and pomegranate seeds | Low GI | V |

SERVES 4

- 2 tbsp olive oil
- 1 red onion, finely chopped
- 2 tsp ground cumin
- 3 garlic cloves, finely chopped
- 1 red chilli
- 1 green chilli
- 2 tbsp passata
- 200g bulghur wheat
- 2 tbsp pomegranate molasses
- 3 tbsp extra virgin olive oil
- 1 tbsp lemon juice
- 5 plum tomatoes, peeled, deseeded and chopped
- 1 bunch of mint, roughly chopped
- 1 small bunch of flat leaf parsley, roughly chopped
- 1 pomegranate, seeds removed

Heat the olive oil in a medium saucepan and saute the onion for 2 to 3 minutes, stirring occasionally. Add the ground cumin, garlic and the chillis and stir well. Cook for a further 2 minutes and then add the passata along with 120ml of water. Bring the mixture to a gentle boil, then remove from the heat and add the bulghur wheat. Put a well fitting lid over the pan and leave it to 'cook' and absorb the liquid, which should take around 15 minutes.

While you are waiting, make the dressing by mixing together the lemon juice, extra virgin olive oil and the pomegranate molasses. Remove the seeds from the pomegranate and set aside, making sure that you don't leave on any of the white pith.

Add the chopped tomato, mint and parsley to the bulghur and fork through gently.

When you are ready to serve, add the dressing to the bulghur, adding carefully as you don't want it to be drenched. Finally scatter over the pomegranate seeds.

Serve with griddled halloumi and lots of green salad.

Hattie Deards

Grilled mackerel with preserved lemons, capers, green olives and parsley | Low GI | GF |

SERVES 4

- 4 fresh mackerel, filleted
- 2 green peppers
- Rind of 2 preserved lemons, diced finely
- small handful of chopped fresh thyme
- 2 heaped teaspoons of capers
- 50g pitted green olives, cut into quarters
- Large handful of fresh flat leaf parsley, chopped finely
- 60ml olive oil
- Sea salt and black pepper

Pre-heat the grill to a high heat. If you do not have a grill, preheat the oven to 220°C.

Grill the green peppers until its skin is blistered, and place it into a plastic bag for a while, until you are able to peel off the skin and remove the seeds. Slice them into strips and set aside.

In a large bowl mix together the strips of pepper, the diced preserved lemon zest, the chopped thyme, the capers, the chopped green olives, parsley and the olive oil. Stir together all the ingredients, and season well with salt and pepper. Taste the salsa again, and add a little more preserved lemon if you feel it is needed.

Line a baking tray with tin foil. Lay out the mackerel fillets next to each other, drizzle over a little olive oil and season with salt and pepper. Cover each fillet with a little salsa, and place the fish under the grill and cook for 3 to 4 minutes, until the fish is just cooked through. If you do not have a grill, bake the fish in the hot oven for approximately 15 minutes, covering it lightly with a little foil.

If you are cooking outside on a bbq, this recipe works perfectly with whole mackerel. Make sure they are gutted and clean, and stuff the fish with the salsa, before seasoning with salt and pepper and drizzling with olive oil on the skin. Cook the mackerel on a hot bbq for 4 minutes on each side, or until cooked through.

Blues

This dish goes well with a large rocket salad and wedges of lemon.

Chicken, sweet potato and cardamom curry | Low GI | GF |

SERVES 4

- 1.1k skinless chicken thighs, off the bone, kept whole or cut into large chunks
- 2 tbsp sunflower oil
- 2 large onions
- 4 large cloves of garlic, finely chopped
- 2 large knobs of fresh ginger, peeled and grated
- 1.5 tsp ground coriander
- 2 tsp ground cumin
- 1 tsp ground cardamom
- 2 level tbsp of mild curry powder
- 500ml chicken stock
- 650g sweet potatoes
- 250 ml natural yoghurt
- 50g of ground almonds
- 1 bunch of fresh coriander leaves and stalks, roughly chopped

You can make this curry with either whole chicken thighs, or cut the thighs into large chunks. Either way, prepare your chicken and set it aside. Finely chop the garlic and grate the ginger, or add both to a food processor and wiz them together. Peel the onions and cut them into sizeable cubes.

Heat the sunflower oil in a large heavy bottomed pan. Gently fry the garlic, grated ginger, the ground coriander, the cumin and the cardamom. Add the onions, stir well and allow to cook for 5 minutes. Add the curry powder, and cook for a further few minutes.

Add the chicken and mix well to ensure that it's covered with the spices and onions. Continue to cook for a further 5 minutes, stirring occasionally to make sure that it doesn't catch on the bottom.

Add the chicken stock, so that it is just covering the meat. Bring the curry to a gentle boil then reduce the heat and allow it to simmer for 10 minutes. If you are using whole chicken thighs, allow them to simmer for 20 minutes instead of 15 minutes.

Peel the sweet potatoes. Cut them in half length ways, and cut on the diagonal into chunks. Add the sweet potatoes to the curry, stir well and simmer for a further 15 minutes with the lid on, until they are 'al dente'.

Mix together the yoghurt and ground almonds in a small bowl, and season well. Roughly chop the coriander, leaves and stalks, and set aside.

When you are ready to eat, scatter over the coriander, and pour over the yoghurt mixture. Alternatively, you can keep the yoghurt in a bowl on the side for people to add if they wish. Serve with rice.

Polly Parsons

GF – ensure that the curry powder and stock are both gluten free.

Cauliflower curry with coriander yoghurt | Low GI | GF |

SERVES 4

- 1 large cauliflower
- 3 tbsp rapeseed oil
- 2 tsp ground turmeric
- 250ml natural yoghurt
- 1 lime
- 2 large bunches of coriander
- 5cm piece of ginger, peeled
- 6 spring onions
- 1 fresh red chilli
- 1 large clove of garlic
- 2 tsp black mustard seeds
- 1 heaped tsp fenugreek seeds
- 1 small handful of curry leaves
- 4 ripe tomatoes
- 1 × 400ml tin of coconut milk
- 200g of fresh pineapple, chopped finely
- 50g flaked almonds
- Sea salt

Pre heat the oven to 220°C.

Cut the outer leaves and the core from the cauliflower. Break the cauliflower into small florets with your hands and place on a large baking sheet or into a large oven dish. Drizzle over one tablespoon of rapeseed oil, sprinkle over a teaspoon of ground turmeric and season with sea salt. Use your hands to mix up the florets of cauliflower, so that they are evenly coated, and put the dish into the oven to cook for 15 minutes or until the cauliflower is just starting to brown but still has a good crunch to it.

Tip the yoghurt into a mixing bowl. Add the zest of half a lime. Roughly chop one bunch of coriander, using just the coriander leaves if you prefer a milder flavour. Mix together the yoghurt, lime zest and coriander and set aside.

Peel the ginger, trim the spring onions and de-seed the chilli. Remove the coriander leaves from the stalks, and peel the garlic. Add the ginger, spring onions, chilli, garlic and coriander stalks to a food processor and whizz them all together.

Heat the remaining two tablespoons of rapeseed oil in a large pan or a deep wok/curry pan. Add the mustard seeds, fenugreek seeds, the remaining teaspoon of turmeric and the curry leaves. Quickly stir together the spices and then add the blended ginger and garlic paste, and stir thoroughly. Allow the paste to cook through for 2 to 3 minutes, until fragrant. Chop the tomatoes, add them to the pan and tip in the coconut milk.

Stir the ingredients over a gentle heat. Tip the tinned pineapple and juice into a blender, chop it into a pulp, and add it to the curry.

Add the roasted cauliflower to the curry and stir. When you are ready to serve dry toast the flaked almonds until they are just golden. Scatter them over the top of the curry, along with fresh coriander leaves. Check the seasoning, and add a squeeze of lime juice if needed.

Serve with wholegrain brown basmati rice, and the coriander yoghurt.

Bridget Gladwin

V (o) – use coconut yoghurt instead of natural yoghurt.
Bridget conjured up this colourful curry after various trips to Kerala. Delicious!

Blueberry, pecan and cardamom muffins | Low GI |

MAKES 12

- 275g wholemeal flour
- 50g broken up pecan nuts
- 1 tsp freshly ground cardamom
- ½ tsp sea salt
- 1.5 tsp baking powder
- ½ tsp bicarbonate of soda
- 35g butter, melted
- 160ml plain yoghurt
- 2 ripe bananas, mashed
- 5 soft dates
- 3 large eggs
- 200g blueberries
- Zest of 1 orange – optional
- Small handful of oats or sugar free muesli

Pre heat the oven to 190°C.

Lay out 12 muffin cases on a baking tray or a muffin tin.

Tip the wholemeal flour into a large mixing bowl. Break up the pecan nuts into sizeable chunks and add them to the bowl, along with the ground cardamom (if you grind up whole cardamom pods, add just the little black seeds that separate from the pod to the muffin) and the sea salt. Add the baking powder and bicarbonate of soda.

Add the butter, yoghurt, bananas, dates and eggs in to a food processor. Whizz them all together and pour the mixture into the bowl with the dry ingredients. Stir together all the ingredients using a metal spoon or spatula, making sure that it is well mixed. Tip in the blueberries and orange zest (if you chose to use it) and give it a final stir.

Spoon the mixture into the muffin cases, distributing it equally.

Sprinkle a few oats or muesli over each muffin, and bake in the oven for 20–25 minutes, or until just firm. If you are unsure whether they are cooked, stick a skewer into the middle of the muffin, and if it comes out clean then you know that they are cooked through.

Hattie Deards

Mango ice cream | Low GI | GF |

- 4 ripe mangoes
- 200ml carton of creamed coconut
- 3 limes

Peel the mangoes and remove the stone. Chop the flesh into a food processor, add the coconut cream and the juice and zest of 2 limes. Blend it all together until absolutely smooth.

Churn the ice cream mixture in an ice cream maker if you have one, otherwise pour into a large plastic tub and place in the freezer. Repeatedly whisk the ice cream mixture with an electric hand beater, always returning the tub to the freezer. It should take around 6 hours to freeze.

Serve the mango ice cream when it's not too hard, and sprinkle the zest of the remaining lime over each serving.

Sarah Willes

Date, polenta, almond and orange cake | Low GI | GF |

- 150g pitted dates
- 270ml sunflower oil
- 220ml of date syrup or maple syrup, or a mix of both
- 2 tsp vanilla extract
- 6 eggs
- 390g ground almonds
- 60g polenta
- 3 tsp baking powder
- Zest of 3 oranges
- Zest of 1 lemon
- Handful of flaked almonds to decorate
- Pre-heat the oven to 140°C.

This cake is a perfect tea time cake – not too sweet and not too over indulgent. It freezes very well and is best eaten after a few days of having been made.

Soak the dates in a bowl of hot water and set aside. Grease and line a large 23cm springform cake tin.

Place the ground almonds, polenta, baking powder, orange and lemon zest into a large mixing bowl and combine well.

Drain the dates and tip them into a food processor or blender. Add the vanilla extract, maple/date syrup and sunflower oil. Blend the ingredients together until they are well combined and a creamy consistency. Pour the mixture into a large mixing bowl, and whisk in the eggs one by one. Add the dry ingredients gradually until they are all combined.

Pour the cake mixture into the cake tin and scatter over the flaked almonds. Place the cake into the oven, and after 25 minutes cover with a layer of tin foil. Bake for a further 45 minutes, or until a skewer comes out clean in the middle.

Alice Dewey

Delphi lodge bread | Low GI |

A perfect bread for people on a yeast free diet, and handily you can freeze the dough.

- 180g strong wholemeal flour
- 50g self-raising flour
- 50g pinhead oatmeal
- 50g wheatgerm
- 50g bran
- 1 tsp baking soda
- ½ tsp salt
- 1 tsp sugar
- 1 egg
- 300ml skimmed milk
- Sunflower seeds, optional

Preheat the oven to 190°C.

Place the dry ingredients in to a large bowl and mix well. Add the egg and milk, and mix together really well with a large spoon.

Spoon the bread mix into a 1lb bread tin, roughly even out the top and sprinkle over the sunflower seeds if you want to use them.

Bake for 45 minutes to 1 hour. Check that the bread is cooked through by inserting a skewer into the middle – it should come out clean when the bread is cooked through.

Clare Latimer

Index

Contributors List

Alice Dewey
Annabel Graham Wood
Ballymaloe Cookery School www.cookingisfun.ie
Blues www.bluesagency.co.uk
Bridget Gladwin www.nutbournevineyards.com
Carina Sage
Clare Latimer www.clareskitchen.co.uk
Darina Allen www.cookingisfun.ie
Dave Renton
Fiona Beckett www.matchingfoodandwine.com
Hattie Deards
Herve Leber
Nama Artisan Raw Foods www.namafoods.com
James Nathan
Jane O'Brien
Kali Hamm www.kalicooking.com
Wild Food Café www.wildfoodcafe.com
Lydia Clark
Oliver Gladwin www.theshed-restaurant.com
Pim Philips
Pip McKellar
Polly Parsons www.hasslefreeweekends.co.uk
Rachel Martino www.byrachelmartino.com
Sam Watherston
Sarah Willes www.bluesagency.co.uk
Stacey Gledhill www.staceygledhill.com
Sybille Pouzet www.sybillepouzet.com
Tanya Maher www.tanyascafe.com
Tim Allen